Rome
Palaces and Gardens

Rome
Palaces and Gardens

SOPHIE BAJARD / RAFFAELLO BENCINI

·TERRAIL·

Frontispiece
The spectacular fountains
at the Villa d'Este, Tivoli.

Cover illustration
The Villa Aldobrandini.

Opposite
Sensual figures painted by Sodoma
in the Alexander and Roxane Room
at the Villa Farnesina.

Editors: Jean-Claude Dubost and Jean-François Gonthier
English Translation: Murray Wyllie
Graphic Design: François Coulibeuf
Art Director: Joseph Dorly
Cover Design: Gérard Lo Monaco and Laurent Gudin
Map: Alexandre Darmon
Typesetting and Filmsetting: D.V. Arts Graphiques, 28000 Chartres
Offset Lithography: Litho Service T. Zamboni, Verona

English edition, copyright © 1997
World copyright © FINEST SA/EDITIONS TERRAIL, PARIS 1997
The Art Book Subsidiary of BAYARD PRESSE SA
Publishing number: 136
ISBN 2-87939-121-0
Printed in Italy

CONTENTS

Opposite
The spectacular well
of the grand spiral staircase
at the Palazzo del Quirinale.

PREAMBLE

It has been my singular good fortune to have lived in Rome and to have experienced the intimate tempo of the city's daily life. The project of writing this book began to take shape while exploring its bustling, sun-bathed streets, streets dominated by the time-worn ochre façades of the Roman palazzi, glowing in the dying rays of sunset. The memory of Rome lies locked away behind these portals, but the tourist, often deterred by their unprepossessing appearance, passes by, little suspecting the hidden splendours contained within. For the secrets of the Roman palazzi are not easily penetrated: their jealous proprietors have chosen to seclude themselves behind somewhat austere façades which discourage the less intrepid. Yet each massive bronze portal stands guard over what is perhaps the most outstanding of all Roman heritages: that of the great aristocratic families whose origins date back to the Middle Ages and who remain, today, proud owners of the family name, titles, land and fortune, playing a leading role in Roman society. It is these great families – the Borghese, Pamphili, Farnese, Medici, Ricci, Ludovisi, Aldobrandini and others – who founded the fortune of the city, who built it stone by stone, from whose ranks sprang great Popes, and who ensured that the Holy See was installed in the heart of the Eternal City. It was furthermore those same families who, from the 16th to the 18th centuries, set the fashion for the country retreat as a means of escaping the stifling summer heat of Rome. They took the rolling vineyards and fortified castles of the Roman campagna surrounding the city *intra-muros* and created magnificent villas such as the Villa d'Este at Tivoli, the Palazzo Farnese at Caprarola, the Villa Lante at Bagnaia and so many others.

Along with Raffaello Bencini, I have penetrated their massive portals, ushering the reader into the privacy of the great families who move in the select circles of the Roman oligarchy and such grand institutions as the Senate, the Presidency of the Republic, the French Academy in Rome, and the French embassies to the Italian Republic and the Holy See.

Pressed for time, the tourist in Rome often misses the opportunity to visit the sumptuous palaces we have described. May this book serve as an inspiration to our readers to set out and discover for themselves these splendid architectural achievements.

Opposite
Caryatids guarding
the nymphaeum spring at the Villa Giulia.

THE ORIGINS
OF THE ROMAN COUNTRY RETREAT

Throughout the Middle Ages, the building of residences beyond the city walls held little appeal for the inhabitants of Rome, owing to relatively low general living standards and to recurrent feuding between local barons. In the city *intra-muros*, cramped conditions meant that people most often made do with a window-ledge pot containing some basil or a few roses, and a fig tree or vine in the corner of a yard. Occasionally, small walled gardens were to be found in monastery cloisters or in castle courtyards.

The first suburban villas made their appearance in the vicinity of Rome in the early 14th century. Internecine feuding began to abate with the end of the papal exile in Avignon and the definitive return of the Holy See to Rome. Wealthier citizens, seeking peace and tranquility, and lulled by soothing ballads and *ritornelli*, gradually adopted a lifestyle more in tune with nature. A passage from Boccaccio's *Decameron*, from the morning of the third day, paints a picture of a typical stately garden of the time. Preferably sited on flat terrain, it is enclosed by high walls, screened by leafy bowers and espaliered fruit trees. Criss-crossed by pergola-shaded alleys and hedge borders, it is laid out around a central lawn of green grass surrounded by rows of orange trees, citrons, palm and pomegranate trees, and boasts a fountain and stone benches. In a corner of the garden lie the flower beds planted with roses, violets, lilies, iris, or more exotic blooms – hyacinths, lilacs and jasmine from far-off Oriental climes. Farther back are to be found the orchard and the *viridarium* with its evergreens, plants such as pines, cypresses, cedars, laurels and olive trees.

The *vigna* may be considered the architectural forerunner of the Roman villa. In the 15th century, most Romans – even the humblest – at least owned a walled *vigna*, consisting of a small *casino*, a garden and, possibly, a few vines. These *vigne* were located on one of the less populated of the seven hills, within the precinct of the Aurelian Wall, or, preferably, beyond the walls along the main roads leading to the city. Vestiges of such *vigne* exist down to this day, mainly behind the Vatican on the slopes of Monte Mario, a stretch of open fields much prized over the centuries and which was to become the choice residential area for wealthy Romans.

Above, and opposite
These plates from *Polyphylia's Dream* depict an ideal 15th-century garden featuring a pergola, espaliered fruit trees and a fountain.

At least twice a year, in late Spring and, particularly, during the grape harvest in September and October, these Romans would forsake their urban palazzi and head for their country houses. During such periods, the city became so deserted that an official decree had to be published pronouncing the suspension of all judicial proceedings during the hottest summer months and the early Autumn.

Some of the larger country residences boasted a tower at each extremity; most, however, consisted of a rectangular two-storey building with a central tower which served both as belvedere and dovecote. Although the plan was highly informal, it was invariably laid out around an interior court, open on three sides and closed on the fourth, for reasons of security, by a fortified wall housing the entrance portal. The sole recurring architectural feature was the ground-floor portico looking out onto a small adjacent garden; this portico was usually supported by octagonal pilasters made from brick or peperino, an omnipresent volcanic rock found in the region around Rome. In similar fashion to the town houses, the façade was often decorated with monochrome paintings or frescoes, or *a graffito* – a technique which consisted of carving images into the wall – and provided with arched or rectangular doors and windows highlighted by plain frames. Not far from the Villa Borghese gardens, Raphael's little *casino*, for instance, conformed to this type. Such buildings were not, strictly speaking, country residences but rather places where family and friends would gather for afternoon relaxation and to dine beneath the vaulted loggia, admiring the view out onto the garden. Abutting the Aurelian Wall, the façades of the *casinos* featured arched windows and, supported by little columns, a small loggia from whence a short flight of steps led down to the flower-beds. Their interior layout resembled one still commonly found in Latium farmhouses, where a ground floor houses the kitchen and storage for farm produce, and an upper-floor bedroom is accessible via an outside staircase.

A RETREAT FOR CHURCH DIGNITARIES

The quintessential feature of such Roman villas was that they were built for senior clergy of the Catholic Church, a characteristic which derived from the extremely ancient division of the Roman society into two distinct civil and religious classes. The election of each new pope – often a foreigner, or an Italian from outside Rome – periodically entailed the mass arrival of immigrant retainers from the homeland or region of the newly-elected pontiff. These newcomers, basking in the favour of their papal compatriot, played an increasingly important role in Roman life: during the reign of the Borgias, for instance, there was a notable influx of Spaniards, while later, under the Medici pontiffs, Florentines flocked to the city. It was above all from the ranks of this new nobility, with its recently-acquired wealth, that patrons were to emerge and develop the architectural type represented by the villa.

The earliest signs of pontifical predilection for country residences had in fact appeared in the High Middle Ages. In the 11th century, Gregory IV was the first pope to settle, not far from the port of Ostia, in a small fortified town which he had himself founded and, in keeping with ancient Roman custom, had proudly named "Gregoriopolis". Throughout the mediaeval period, successive popes sought refuge in the rolling hills of the Roman campagna, perhaps motivated more by considerations of security than the desire for mere leisure. Thus, in times of turmoil, the Holy See, along with its various administrative departments, would periodically be transferred to the temporary safety of outlying towns such as Viterbo, Bomarzo or

Bagnaia where the pope usually resided in the episcopal palace or local monastery. Following the return of the papacy to Rome in 1420, after the "Babylonian Captivity" in Avignon, Martin V launched the vogue for the country residence at Tivoli, which, throughout the entire 15th century, was to be the favourite retreat for popes and cardinals. For humanist writers and artists, Tivoli's appeal lay not merely in its pleasant climate and the presence of their major patrons, but also in the ubiquitous vestiges of classical antiquity that studded the landscape.

In those days, the official duration of the pontifical retreat was not governed by the necessities of agriculture, but by the progress of the season, and the liturgical calendar of the Church. A papal tradition developed whereby the cardinals resident in the Vatican were authorised to take their leave of the court throughout the summer months. During the Renaissance, this vacation period tended to be extended, often beyond reasonable bounds. As a rule, the recess began on the feast of St Peter, on 29 June, and court activities resumed in the city on All Saints' day, on 1 November. Before long, many cardinals were taking advantage of the four-month vacation period to set about building villas in the vicinity of Rome.

In the early 16th century, Pope Julius II apparently took particular pleasure in escaping from the stultifying atmosphere of the Vatican palace to spend the evening – and even occasionally the night – at the home of his friend Agostino Chigi, who had recently commissioned a splendid suburban villa, the Farnesina.

Above
Located in the very heart of Tivoli, the Villa d'Este, its façade partially concealed by a row of cypress trees, bathes in the soft light of the setting sun.

Left
The houses of Bomarzo clustering on the hillside.

Opposite
The fortified citadel of Bagnaia nestling beneath the high tower of the castle.

Above
Peruzzi's fine classical façade
at the Villa Farnesina.

The Villa Farnesina

Chigi had arrived in Rome from his native Siena and soon became accredited banker to Popes Alexander VI and Leo X. Skilfully managing his banking activities and his revenue from the Tolfa alum mines, he gradually built up a vast financial empire, operating a fleet of some hundred ships that ceaselessly plied the Mediterranean as far as the Levant. Chigi became so powerful that, in 1506, Julius II decided to ennoble him, marrying him into the papal family, the Della Rovere, and thus entitling the banker to emblazon the Della Rovere oak tree emblem on the Chigi arms, which show six golden mountains surmonted by a star.

In 1505, the man univcrsally known in Rome as "Il Magnifico" acquired a plot of land on the left bank of the Tiber beyond the Porta Settimiana – in those days a sparsely populated area – and immediately commissioned his compatriot, the famous Sienese architect Baldassare Peruzzi, to build a residence befitting his new status.

Peruzzi chose brick, a commonly-employed material in Sienese architecture, for the new palace, enhancing this brickwork by the addition of traditional Roman peperino stone which he used to highlight the horizontal and vertical lines wall base, cornice, pilaster bases of the capitals, and quoins, of his delicate composition. The façade of the two-storey building features rhythmical rows of elegant Tuscan pilasters; the upper storey is highlighted by a stucco frieze of bas-relief

Top
The quartered coat of arms of the Chigi, emblazoned in the stucco vault of the staircase leading to the first floor.

putti tugging gaily at garlands of fruits between which are set small attic windows.

From an architectural point of view, the Villa Farnesina may be regarded as the most accomplished example of the 15th-century villa. Its plan consists of a main block, flanked by two north-facing projecting wings surrounding a large ground-floor loggia. Quite unusually for a Roman villa, this loggia was formerly the main entrance to the building and thus, rather than facing onto the street as was normally the case, lay parallel to it. Although the villa's entrance portal did indeed give onto the street, it was set back considerably to the north in such a way that the main alley leading to the loggia lay in exact alignment to the former. By detaching the villa from its principal access-way, Peruzzi invested it with an intimate, secluded atmosphere. Originally, the east façade looking out onto the Tiber also opened onto gardens via a second loggia. Beneath the shade of a vine-covered pergola, an alley led through planted beds of violets, roses and lilacs, bordered by lemon trees, towards the tree-lined river bank. By the river, a loggia with a basement wine-cellar was laid out for banquets on summer evenings.

Agostino Chigi, a connoisseur patron, commissioned the most fashionable artists of the day – Raphael, Peruzzi, Sodoma and Sebastiano del Piombo – to glorify his own person in a

Above
The inside shutters in the rooms embellished with delicately executed paintings.

Opposite
Grotesque and mythological scenes alternate on the coffered ceiling in the Alexander and Roxane bedroom.

Top right hand page
The 18th-century façade of the Palazzo Corsini standing opposite the villa.

Bottom right hand page
The villa with its ornamental fountain nestling in a bower of greenery.

decorative scheme drawn up for both exterior and interior of the villa. The façade of the loggia was covered with sanguine-tinted chiaroscuro frescoes executed by Peruzzi himself, of which nothing save the occasional female figure bearing a cornucopia survives. Peruzzi was also responsible for the paintings in three other rooms in the villa. The vaulted ceiling of the Galatea loggia, which formerly opened onto the gardens, is covered with constellations and zodiacal signs positioned according to Agostino Chigi's astrological chart, which proclaims his birth under a configuration of lucky stars. The mythological creatures depicted in the lunettes, as well as the awesome *Polyphemus* adorning one of the walls, were painted by the Venetian Sebastiano del Piombo, while the beautiful

Above
In a recessed wall niche, Venus crouches beside her incorrigible suitor Cupid.

Opposite
Raphael's *Galatea* proudly riding the waves amidst tritons and other marine creatures.

Right hand page
On the walls of the Galatea loggia, 17th-century trompe-l'œil landscapes recreate the illusion of a space formerly opening onto the gardens.

Previous pages (pp. 18-19)
Peruzzi designed the Perspectives Room as a trompe-l'œil belvedere offering a panoramic vista of the city and nearby countryside.

Galatea, emerging half-naked from the waves, is the work of the great Raphael. The overall theme of the fresco suite celebrates the four realms of the universe: the Heavens on the ceiling, the Air in the lunettes, the Waters in the *Galatea* and, finally, the Earth, embodied in the villa itself.

The four walls of the first-floor salon display trompe-l'œil architectural settings in which multiple perspective effects are created by illusionary loggias which follow the oblique line of the walls and from which can be admired the distant panorama of equally illusionary landscapes. This salon leads to the master bedroom, painted from floor to ceiling by the Sienese Sodoma with epic scenes portraying Alexander the Great, intended to echo episodes from Agostino Chigi's own life. Thus the *Marriage of Alexander and Roxane* is an allusion to Chigi's own marriage to his young bride, Francesca Ordeaschi, whom he had brought back from Venice. The tremulously joyful theme of love and sensuality is pursued in the decorated vaulted ceiling in the main loggia, where plump gods and goddesses, executed from the artist's drawings by Raphael's regular assistants, Giulio Romano, Francesco Penni and Giovanni da Udine, depict the legend of the fair Psyche and her lover Cupid.

A villa devoted to pleasure, the fruit of amorous whim, the Farnesina was sold by the Chigi heirs in the late 16th century to Cardinal Alessandro Farnese, from whom it derives its present name. Transferred, along with all the other Farnese possessions, to the Bourbons of Naples, the villa was subsequently sold to the Italian State. In 1929, it became the seat of the Accademia Nazionale dei Lincei and is now open to the public.

Above
Sodoma's colourful frescoes extolling the exemplary life of Alexander the Great echo that of the artist's patron, Chigi.

Opposite
A glimpse of the villa's façade framed by the large conifers in the garden.

Right hand page
In a gesture of passionate love, Alexander the Great offers his crown to his voluptuous slave Roxane, teased by mischievous *putti*.

THE PLEASURES OF THE HUNT

Paolo Uccello, *The Hunt in the Forest*
c. 1460, oil on wood, 73 × 177 cm. (29 × 70 in.)
Ashmolean Museum, Oxford.

From the late 15th century onwards, the inhabitants of Rome would often be greeted by the sight of brightly-dressed bands of hunters, riding out from the city to the nearby domains of La Magliana and Campo di Merlo where Count Girolamo Riario, the nephew of Pope Sixtus IV, hosted spectacular hunting parties, which usually culminated in improvised alfresco banquets where the game that had been bagged was served to the guests.

The Venetian Cardinal-Chamberlain Lodovico Trevisan was probably responsible for introducing the vogue for hunting into Roman aristocratic and senior ecclesiastical circles. Although, since the High Middle Ages, the clergy had been forbidden by canon law to hunt, they were themselves members of a noble caste for whom the sport represented a peacetime substitute for martial activities. Cardinal Trevisan, aptly nicknamed "cardinal Lucullus", was the first ecclesiastical

dignitary to dare breed hounds and horses specifically for hunting purposes. The packs – greyhounds, harriers and setters – usually hailed from the renowned kennels of Ferraras where, for over a century, the lords of Lombardy had been keen practitioners of the hunt.

In late 15th-century Rome, the great aristocratic hunter was apparently Cardinal Ascanio Sforza, the Duke of Milan's brother, who introduced the enclosed game reserve modelled on the great North Italian game parks, or *barchi*. In actual fact, such game reserves had been fashionable in ancient Rome where a *vivarium*, or kind of breeding park for wild animals destined for the circus games, had been situated near to the baths of Diocletian. A wild animal park, much appreciated by the Roman nobility, remained in the area until the 16th century.

Originally, the La Magliana hunting lodge had been used as a stopping-place by Pope Innocent VIII on his frequent boat trips down to Ostia where he would bless the fleet as they set off to engage the Turks in the Mediterranean. Moreover, it was in the course of the war against the Infidels that La Magliana began to assume the role it was to play for centuries. In 1482, Prince Djem, the brother of the Sultan of Turkey, was captured by papal troops and held as a valuable hostage. As the Prince was a highly accomplished horseman, great hunting expeditions were organised at La Magliana to provide distraction during his captivity.

In the early 16th century, the great humanist Pope Leo X also enjoyed partaking in the joys of the hunt, particularly appreciating its meticulously planned ceremonial aspects. The day before the hunt proper, professional hunters would set off to reconnoitre the land and mark out a wooded zone with strips of cloth. The following day, the papal party would arrive and the pope himself would choose a high vantage point from which he could admire the spectacle. The hounds, led by local peasants and the Swiss Guards, then drove the game – usually deer, wild boar or rabbit – into the demarcated area. Later, falcons would be unleashed on the smaller game and birds raised in the papal aviary. It was in his hunting lodge that, in 1521, Leo X contracted the fever to which he was to succumb a few days later in the Vatican.

NON HVMILIS VOBIS BALNEARIA LAVDIBVS VLLIS
CERTAT NON VESTRAS AEMVLA IACTAT OPES
AT SIMILEM VOBIS DOMINVM SI NACTA FVISSET
ISSET ET IPSA ALIQVO FORSAN HABENDA LOCO

The great *barchi* at Caprarola, Bagnaia and Tivoli

The passion for hunting continued unabated throughout the 16th century, even at the height of the Counter-Reformation. Cardinals such as Carlo Carafa, nephew of the forbidding Paul IV, Ferdinand de' Medici, Jean Du Bellay, Alessandro Farnese and Ippolito II d'Este were all widely reputed as keen hunters. It was men like these who created the *barchi*, the great Renaissance game reserves at Bagnaia, Tivoli and Caprarola.

The first great *barco* to appear in the vicinity of Rome was that of Bagnaia in the early 16th century. Cardinal Raffaele Riario, appointed Bishop of Viterbo, was captivated by the castle of Bagnaia and made it his summer residence. From 1514, on the wooded slopes of Monte Sant'Angelo above the town, he laid out a game reserve and had built a small hunting lodge, which also served for the traditional banquets following the hunt. Throughout the first half of the 16th century, the bishops of Viterbo enthusiastically availed themselves of the new amenity, but it was not until the latter half of the century that Cardinal Gambara decided to build the splendid Villa Lante on the site, retaining only one wooded area of the original reserve, transforming the former park into a traditional *bosco* which extended beyond the villa gardens.

A similar fate was reserved for the two Tivoli game parks which, in 1560, Cardinal Ippolito d'Este decided to lay out on the lands surrounding his sumptuous villa. Between the castle of Tivoli and the San Giovanni church, he closed off a first park, known as a *barchetto*, for small game and exotic fauna. A larger reserve, the *barco* proper, was then laid out on the marshy plain below Tivoli along the bank of the Aniene, and it was there that the cardinal held spectacular big game hunts. On the site of a former Roman quarry, the cardinal's architect built a hunting lodge – a massive, compact building topped by a central belvedere, containing apartments for the exclusive use of the proprietor. Following the death of the cardinal, the lands were restored to the town of Tivoli.

The immense *barco* which, in turn, Cardinal Alessandro Farnese commissioned in 1569 near his new residence, a mile or two from the town of Caprarola, was not destined to outlive its owner either. Over a mile and a half in circumference, the park teemed with a huge variety of wild animals and included woodland, areas of pasture and a lake. On a promontory above the lake stood a two-storey hunting lodge which Vignola, architect of the palazzo at Caprarola, had surmounted with a central belvedere provided with three windows on each side and crowned by a dovecote. The park, abandoned by the family heirs, was eventually acquired by the town of Caprarola.

The late 16th century witnessed a marked decline in the vogue for hunting, and it lost its place as the preferred sport of the Roman nobility. The introduction of firearms in the latter half of the century was a major factor in the extinction of larger game, and the feasibility of laying out vast reserves was restricted by the sheer number of country residences now being built. A period of lasting peace had been ushered in and the nobility, no longer requiring an outlet for pent-up martial inclinations, found more enjoyable distraction in the theatre or, with the coming of the baroque, in the opera.

THE VILLA, MIRROR OF ANTIQUITY

The coming of more peaceful times led to the construction of ever more villas. In the opening decades of the 16th century, when topographical research into ancient Rome was making great strides thanks to the study of antique ruins, an increasing number of excavations, and the activities of antiquaries who zealously tracked down any object related to the classical past to add to their collections, an attempt was made to rediscover the architectural laws as defined by the ancients. In pursuit of an authentic image of the ideal villa, scholars delved into Pliny's letters – where the author boasts to a friend of the charms of his houses in Laurentum and Tuscany – or the ten volumes of Vitruvius' *De Architectura*, and enthusiastically explored the ruins of Hadrian's palatial residence at Tivoli, as well as other still-extant ancient villas on the Pincio.

From the latter villas, still standing at the time of the Renaissance, 16th-century architects borrowed the formal style in which vaulted ceilings were subdivided into octagonal, hexagonal or triangular compartments, or into lunettes – a variant known as the pendentive vault. Grotesques and stucco relief work were used to frame painted scenes, usually depicting classical themes taken from Ovid's *Metamorphoses*, Apuleius, or the myth of the founding of Rome. Humanists and scholars turned to classical literature in order to devise iconographic programmes appropriate to the clients' wishes, and painters then followed those meticulous schemes to the letter.

That classical influence on Roman villa architecture proved a decisive factor, and was to remain so for centuries to come. It was to find its most concrete expression in the early 16th century, in the designs drawn up by Bramante for the Cortile del Belvedere at the Vatican, and by Raphael for the Villa Madama.

Like Bramante, Raphael drew inspiration from the study of ancient monuments. Appointed Superintendent of Roman Antiquities by Leo X, he was able to devote himself to a minute examination of the past, combing the streets of Rome in pursuit of topographical details which would enable him to draw up a map of the city as it had stood in classical times. In the course of his exploratory work, accompanied by his inseparable assistant Giovanni da Udine, he led an archeological expedition into the subterranean ruins of Nero's famous *Domus Aurea* on Monte Oppius near the Colosseum.

Top left hand and right hand pages
Renaissance artists were fascinated by the ruins of the Great Baths and the ornamental Canope pool at the Villa Hadriana at Tivoli.

Above and opposite
The 16th century rediscovered the alternating stucco reliefs and grotesques which embellished classical vaults.

Raphael was so impressed by his visit to those ruins – referred to by contemporaries as grottos, hence the coining of the term "grotesque" to describe the decorative frescoes found there – that in his subsequent villas grotesque motifs formed the sole decorative features, covering entire surfaces of the vaulted ceilings and the walls.

Giovanni da Udine, for his part, succeeded, after much trial and error, in reproducing the process for making white stucco – a mixture of lime and pulverised marble – used to create the subtle reliefs he had admired on the vaults of Nero's Golden House, and which he himself was to use extensively when working with Raphael, particularly in the loggia at the Villa Madama.

In the original plans drawn up by Raphael,
the curious hemicycle of the uncompleted
façade of the Villa Madama was intended
to form the building's internal atrium.

The Villa Madama

In 1516, Leo X issued a papal bull to facilitate the suburban development of Rome. The decree extended the privileges already granted by his predecessors promoting development within the city of Rome, and as a result, cardinals were encouraged to commission the building of suburban residences. Shortly after the promulgation of the bull, the Villa Madama was designed for the pope's cousin Cardinal Giulio de' Medici, by Raphael, and it provided a classically inspired model which came to define the very type of the Renaissance villa.

Cardinal de' Medici chose to build his country house to the north of the Vatican, on the lush green slopes of Monte Mario, which is still today a highly sought-after district of Rome. Although works commenced in 1518, supervised by Raphael who had designed an extremely ambitious project for the cardinal, the construction of the villa met with repeated setbacks and the project was never completed. On the sudden death of the architect in 1520, his fine project was left in the hands of his leading assistant, Antonio da Sangallo the Younger, who had worked with him at St Peter's. The following year, the death of Leo X led to the disgrace of Cardinal de' Medici, and the latter had to seek refuge in Florence. Works ground to a halt, then resumed in 1524 when the cardinal, in turn, was elected pope as Clement VII.

However, when the Imperial troops swept into Rome in 1527, they set fire to the building which was still under construction, causing considerable damage. Clement VII

looked on resignedly as the flames blazed higher in his villa; Cardinal Colonna, at the head of the Imperial armies, was exacting revenge on the pope for having despoiled him of his own possessions. The sack of Rome put paid to all hope of seeing Raphael's project materialised, and with the exception of a few subsequent minor alterations, the villa today remains frozen in the same state of incompletion as it was in the aftermath of 1527.

Raphael, applying the principles laid down by Vitruvius in his ten-volume treatise *De Architectura*, apparently paid particular attention to providing the various rooms in the house with an orientation appropriate to their function and to the changing seasons. Accordingly, the building was laid out along a longitudinal axis running from south-east to north-west, parallel to the hillside. The villa had two openings onto the city; the first, to the south-east, was accessible via the road from the Vatican; the second, centrally located at the base of the north-east façade, lay in the axis of the road which ascended Monte Mario from the Ponte Milvio across the Tiber to the north of Rome. The ensemble formed an impressive five hundred and eighty-foot long rectangular block surrounded by a wall provided with four round corner-towers.

Left hand page
At the end of the first wall enclosing the ornamental Italian parterre, Bandinelli's twin colossi guard the entrance to the hippodrome.

Opposite
On the wall of the fishpond, Giovanni da Udine's realistically sculpted head of Leo X's court mascot, the elephant Annone, a gift from the King of Portugal.

Left hand page
The impressive triple-vaulted
elevation of the loggia looking
onto the gardens is worthy
of a cathedral nave.

Above
This frieze by Giulio Romana features
a rhythmical composition
of Winged Victories in flowing robes,
large festoons, and chubby *putti*.

The first entrance door led into an imposing vestibule which in turn led to a space described by Raphael as the "atrium". This atrium, its circular shape derived from Greek architecture, formed the nucleus of the villa around which the reception rooms were distributed. To either side of these salons lay the private rooms proper. The cardinal's winter apartments faced south so that the rooms could benefit from the warmth of any available sunlight, whereas the summer apartments faced north. The latter opened onto a monumental loggia overlooking the gardens which culminated in a grand exedra facing the hill. Below the gardens lay a large terraced fishpond, a cool refreshing spot offering respite from the summer heat.

The only parts of that ambitious complex to be completed were the north apartments, the loggia and the gardens. The large circular courtyard was only half completed, hence the highly unusual semi-circular façade of the present-day building. Nowadays, the entrance leads into a vestibule adjacent to the apartments providing direct access to the loggia. Even in its present truncated form, the villa, with its rigorous design and delicate proportions, retains a remarkable force which undoubtedly impressed those who saw it when it was being built.

The monumentally proportioned loggia, with its ceiling of alternate central domes and lateral ribbed vaults revealing ethereal arcades, is reminiscent of a previous loggia designed by Raphael at the Vatican Palace. As at the Vatican, Raphael's two principal assistants for the paintings were Giulio Romano and the painter-architect Baldassare Peruzzi, while Giovanni da Udino executed the stucco decorations. Both walls and vaulted ceilings literally teem with grotesques inspired by mediaeval bestiaries and floral miscellanies, and the intensive use of the grotesque here was to decisively influence future fresco decoration. The paintings on the vaulted ceilings depict fables from Ovid's *Metamorphoses*, an inexhaustible fount of inspiration for Renaissance artists, while the white walls, embellished by stucco reliefs, feature rows of niches that formerly housed classical statuary.

The cardinal was proud of the gushing fountains in the gardens, and in particular of his nymphaeum, located in a hollow on the hillside to the north-west of the hippodrome at the end of the garden. The plans of both the nymphaeum and the network of ornamental fountains – including Giovanni da

Above
The Medici coat of arms with its six
palle, beneath which is inscribed
the allegory of Night capped
by a lunar crescent.

Opposite
The upper bays of Giulio Romana's
vaulted ceiling are strewn with
delicate, subtly painted grotesques
highlighting Cardinal Giulio
de' Medici's family motto.

Udine's famous Elephant Fountain – were designed by Antonio da Sangallo. All that remains of the ornamental statuary formerly found in the park are Bandinelli's stucco colossi guarding the entrance portal to the hippodrome.

Following the death of Clement VII, the villa was acquired by the Medici family, and it became home above all to the daughter of Emperor Charles V, Margaret of Austria, known as Madama, who inherited the property on the death of her husband, Duke Alessandro de' Medici, and who gave it her name. Remarried, this time to Duke Ottavio Farnese, grandson of Paul III, Margaret often organised festivities there in honour of the pope who appears to have been particularly attracted to the villa. In 1555, ownership of the villa accordingly passed from the Medici to the Farnese and it remained in possession of Farnese cardinals throughout the latter half of the 16th century. Left in a state of relative neglect by the Bourbons of Naples, it was only intermittently occupied until its purchase in 1940 by the Italian government, since when it has been used as a conference centre and official residence for foreign VIP guests.

Left hand page
On the loggia vaults, painted stuccos and frescoes form a harmonious ensemble, the joint creation of Giulio Romana and Giovanni da Udine.

Below
One of the many classical sarcophagi from Cardinal de' Medici's collection which still embellish the garden paths today.

The Palazzo Madama

The same Margaret of Austria also left her mark on the palace which the Medici had commissioned in the very centre of Rome, a stone's throw from the Piazza Navona and the church of S. Luigi de' Francesi. At the beginning of the 16th century, the glorious Palazzo Madama was merely a small residence, built by Sinulfo di Castell'Ottieri, treasurer to Sixtus IV, on a plot that had been sold off by the French community. On Sinulfo's death in 1505, the house was bought by Cardinal Giovanni de' Medici, son of Lorenzo the Magnificent. It was not until 1513 that the cardinal, following his elevation to pontifical office as Leo X, at last set about converting the property into a residence worthy of his new status, commissioning the Florentine architect Giuliano da Sangallo, who had often worked for the Medici, to design the project for his new palace.

In the original building, two series of apartments were distributed around a central courtyard onto which, on all four sides, opened the grand arcades of the loggia. Sangallo initially intended to extend the main group of buildings by two portico wings with a raised parterre linking the palace and the Piazza Navona. This ambitious project, never realised, seemingly prefigures the two wings which Bernini was to design for Alexander VII in front of St Peter's. Following on from Bramante and Raphael, Sangallo also demonstrated his intention to revive the architectural tenets laid down by classical antiquity.

Left hand page
The main courtyard of the Palazzo Madama, redesigned in the 17th century, still retains the original ground-floor portico dating from the era of Leo X.

The 17th-century arcaded
courtyard with its rows
of senatorial busts,
incorporating to the right
the mediaeval Crescenzi tower.

Opposite
The frescoes embellishing the walls
and vaulted ceiling of the Pannini Room
offer an audacious display of Baroque
delight in trompe-l'œil architectural
effects.

Above
The sumptuously decorated ceiling
of the Maccari Room, a late
19th-century tribute to the glory
of the Senate, featuring frescoes
executed in a typically romantic vein.

Opposite
The 17th-century frieze
in the Marconi Room
with its rhythmical succession
of massive allegories.

It was in one of the rooms of the Palazzo Madama that the priceless volumes from Lorenzo the Magnificent's library were finally to be displayed. The collection had been dispersed in 1494 during the Medici exile from Florence when the young Cardinal Giovanni, disguised as a monk to escape the wrath of the Florentines, had fled to Venice, taking with him part of the much-prized collection. Moreover, in a small garden adjacent to the palace, he installed his collection of classical marbles unearthed in the course of the numerous excavations he had commissioned in the city. The doors of the Palazzo Madama were graciously thrown open to artists and scholars and it swiftly became a forum for Roman humanist culture.

By law, the young Catharine de' Medici ought to have inherited the palace; however, in 1533, Clement VII cheated her out of her rightful inheritance, transferring it to his son, Duke Alessandro, in exchange for the dowry which the hapless Catharine received for her marriage to the Dauphin of France. When, shortly after, Alessandro was assassinated by his cousin, the notorious Lorenzaccio immortalized in the play by de Musset, the family palace passed into the hands of his foreign widow, Margaret of Austria, who managed to expunge all trace of the Medici name. She lived in the palace for many years, refusing to share the same roof as her new husband, Duke Ottavio Farnese, whom she wholeheartedly detested. On her death, the Medici resumed ownership of the property. Work had been begun on a second conversion project in the days of Grand Duke Cosimo II, but a third, definitive project, drawn up by the architect Paolo Marucelli, was commissioned by Ferdinand II in 1642.

Although Ferdinand II displayed neither great ambition nor firm political resolve in running the Medici State which languished under his rule, he did, on the other hand, leave his mark as an outstanding patron of the arts and literature and was responsible for the acquisition of many of the works of art that form the nucleus of the Pitti and Uffizi collections. The baroque façade of the palace was divided into three orders of nine windows, highlighted by refined frames crowned by alternate rectangular, arched or triangular tympana. The frames rest on elegant consoles and are flanked by slender caryatid figures. The upper storey is surmounted by a mezzanine with small attic windows framed by a frieze of bas-relief *putti* carrying, as at the Villa Farnesina, garlands of fruits, and the ensemble is topped by an imposing cornice.

The vestibule leads into the main courtyard with its six ethereal columns and fine paving of polychrome cipollino-marble slabs retrieved from excavations in the city. To the left of the portico, Marucelli's sweeping grand staircase is built on the base of the former stairs designed by Sangallo. Several fine 16th-century coffered ceilings painted with floral motifs and embellished with gold leaf are still to be found on the first floor, such as that in the Signatura Room boasting a delicate frieze of intertwining *putti*, fruits and flowers, in the Mazzini Room, the centre ceiling of which displays an ostrich, the traditional symbol of resolution and strength, and in the staircase of S. Luigi de' Francesi bearing the Medici seal. To this initial nucleus of Medici appartments were added several rooms in which the 17th-century friezes executed during the renovation of the palace have survived to this day; one such is the Marconi Room, decorated with scenes from the life of Cardinal Alessandro de' Medici who, in 1605, reigned briefly as Leo XI.

In 1753, the grand duchy of Tuscany, along with all its possessions including the Palazzo Madama, passed to the House of Lorraine. Two years later, Pope Benedict XIV bought back the building which became the seat of papal government. From a private residence, that tangible expression of Medici power was thus transformed into a public palace. The final blow came in 1849, when Pius IX decided to accommodate the Finance Ministry offices in the building. When Rome was made capital of a united Italian State in 1871,

Above
The baroque façade of the palace is embellished with numerous relief motifs such as this lion's head girdling the window frame.

Opposite
One of the ground-floor "kneeling" windows, so called because of the inverted "S" shape of the supporting consoles.

Left hand page
The fine coffered ceiling of the Mazzini Room, with its central ostrich figure symbolising resolution, dates from the time of Margaret of Austria.

Above and opposite
The frieze in the Marconi Room
with its alternate allegories and scenes
from the life of Alessandro de' Medici.

Right hand page
The triumphant allegory of Aurora
suffused in sunlight on the ceiling
of the Pannini Room.

the Palazzo Madama became seat of the Senate and has remained so ever since.

The 16th century villas not only borrowed from the architectural and pictorial typology of classical monuments; they also borrowed vestiges of ancient Rome in a more literal sense, deliberately incorporating them on site. Many villas made use of the old Aurelian walls as an enclosure delimiting their land. And, on the slopes of the Palatine hill, the still-intact vestiges of the illustrious monuments which had once stood in the bustling heart of the ancient city were harmoniously incorporated into the Orti Farnesiani.

51

The Orti Farnesiani

In 1567, Vignola designed the Orti Farnesiani complex for Cardinal Alessandro Farnese on the ruins of Tiberius's palace overlooking the Roman Forum. The architect achieved a spectacular blend between the classical monuments of both the Roman and Palatine forums, and Cardinal Farnese's terraced gardens which ran down to the very foot of Maxentius' basilica. Built on the hill slope on successive tiers linked by flights of steps and embellished with fountains, the layout of the terraced gardens is breathtakingly dramatic. Originally, an imposing rustic portal – nowadays moved to the side entrance of the Palatine Forum – marked the passage between the two forums. This triumphal arch formerly served as façade to a vestibule stretching along the boundary wall.

The vestibule led to the esplanade of a vast exedra, from which a main ramp, flanked by two other narrower ramps, led to the *casino*. The main ramp ascended in gradual flights to a first loggia housing the Rain Nymphaeum, so called because of the water which dripped profusely from the stalactites onto visitors' heads. The two more steeply-inclined lateral ramps led directly to the second terrace from whence a single central stair climbed to the third level, the only one to have survived.

Two overhanging terraces, laid out on either side of the stairs, offer a panoramic view of the gardens on the slopes of the Palatine hill. The vast esplanade preceding the terraces looks onto the fountain basin and, in the background, the large

Left hand page
The parterres in the hanging gardens which stretch to the Palatine Forum, filled with the bitter-sweet scent of orange and lemon trees.

Opposite
One of the small twin *casini*, designed as loggias offering views out over Rome – glimpsed through the wrought-iron grating – and onto the parterres to the rear.

Below
Along one of the stairways leading to the pavilions, partially screened in a leafy acanthus bower, a winged griffon keeps a watchful eye on visitors.

Previous pages (pp. 52-53)
The view from the terraces of the Orti Farnesiani takes in the Roman Forum with, in the background, the rectangular Tabularium building beyond which lies the Capitol square.

Opposite
The Roman Forum seen from the Orti
Farnesiani, with, in the foreground,
San Lorenzo in Miranda church built
on the foundations of the temple
of Antoninus and Faustina.

Below
Sheltered from the wind by the aviaries,
Cardinal Farnese enjoyed dining
on the terrace of the gardens amidst
the murmuring fountains.

Right hand page
Alongside the waterfall basin,
one of the two staircases leading
to the pavilions.

niche hollowed into the base of the *casino* with its roaring
waterfall. Finally, flights of stairs lead, on either side of the
basin, to the last terrace located on the same level as the
entrance proper to the pavilions. These twin *casini*, separated
by an ultimate central terrace and originally surmounted by
wrought-iron cupolae, are actually aviaries. They were added
to Vignola's original project by the baroque architect Girolamo
Rainaldi at the end of the 16th century. Positioned slightly
aslant of the main axis to avoid creating an excessively symmetrical effect, they are provided with large openings on all
sides and offer a 360-degree panoramic view onto the gardens,
the city and the surrounding hills.

Behind the two aviaries, the criss-crossing parterres of
the gardens stretch out like an immense floral carpet. Planted
with rare and exotic species, they were formerly one of the
richest botanical gardens in Italy, with ornamental statuary,
bas-reliefs and antique marbles transferred from the nearby

Previous pages (pp. 58-59)
On the grounds of the Palatine Forum,
this huge rectangular space known
as Emperor Domitian's stadium
was in fact a hippodrome.

Coliseum to the summit of the Palatine hill. In the late 17th century, they were occasionally used for evening theatrical performances given by the Arcadians, a company of poet-shepherds seeking a lost Arcadia, who adopted the delightful spot with its haunting memories of classical antiquity.

The Orti Farnesiani passed from the House of Farnese to the Bourbons who tranferred the classical statuary and marbles to Naples, linked the twin aviaries by a loggia, and replaced the cupolae by building a single roof over the two *casini*. Unfortunately, as a result of the excavations carried out by the city of Rome, present-day proprietor of the gardens, the terraces were largely demolished in the 19th century. Nevertheless, the Palatine hill still offers one of the most pleasant walks in Rome and the panoramic view over the city remains breathtakingly beautiful.

Left hand page
Along the garden paths, murmuring fountains and large shaded pine trees offer a cool respite from the summer sun.

Opposite
In the days of the Farnese, classical statuary embellished the niches in this shaded grotto.

THE VIA GIULIA, A ROMAN SHOWCASE

When Julius II gave Bramante a free hand to design the Villa Belvedere courtyard at the Vatican, the gesture was simply one part of an ambitious renovation project for Rome *intra-muros*, which was to see work commence on the most magnificent palaces of the great Roman families. Since the late 15th century, the Arenula district, hugging the bend in the Tiber between the Tiberine Island and the Vatican, had become the focal link between the Trastevere and the Sant'Eustachio customs barrier, the University and the Piazza Navona market. Three bustling major thoroughfares wound through the district, linking the various other parts of the city, and all converging at the Ponte San Angelo: the Via Papale coming from the Lateran, the Via Recta which began not far from the Piazza Capranica and, finally, the Via Peregrinorum which started out at the Octavian Portico, near the Theatre of Marcellus. The old Roman families, thanks to a papal bull issued by Sixtus IV authorising the owner of a well-maintained residence to progressively buy up neighbouring derelict property, had their palaces built along these main routes.

To counter the hegemony of this old Roman oligarchy, and to bestow favours on families which rallied to his own camp, Julius II was to open up a new axis running along the banks of the Tiber parallel to the river. It soon came to be known as the Via Giulia, and its rectilinear alignment offered a stark contrast to the other winding mediaeval streets. That new commercial thoroughfare provided a rapid link between the Tiberine Island – and its quays where ships' cargos were unloaded – and the papal city. Julius II also undertook renovation works in the immediate vicinity of the Via Giulia aimed at making the area more practicable: the narrow winding 13th-century streets were widened and straightened, and irregularly laid-out, ill-defined squares, such as the Campo dei Fiori and the Piazza Capodiferro, were re-designed on a more symmetrical basis in relation to the axis of the streets. Papal administrative departments moved into buildings along the Via Giulia, while the families newly ennobled by the pope and won over to his cause built their palaces there. The new street was swiftly to become the dazzling showcase of Rome, a hub of perpetual display.

Veduta di Ponte Sisto

... *le di S Cecilia 3 Camp di S Grisogono 4 Camp di S Sabina sul Monte Aventino 5 Camp di S Maria in Cosmedin 6 Orti Farnesi alla Longara*

Left hand page
The rectilinear alignment
of the Via Giulia offered a striking
contrast to the fabric of mediaeval
Rome with its narrow winding
streets.

Above
In the 16th century, boats sailing
upstream from the coast would
unload their cargos on the banks
of the Tiberine Island; the goods
would then be taken to the Vatican
along the newly-built Via Giulia.

The Palazzo Farnese

The Palazzo Farnese was the first new residence built along the Via Giulia. In 1495, Cardinal Alessandro Farnese decided to acquire the former residence of the Spanish Cardinal Pedro Ferriz, the main façade of which had stood since the late 15th century on the Via della Regola, the key thoroughfare running through the city centre in mediaeval times. Initially, the young cardinal did no more than carry out repairs to his newly-acquired property. Soon, however, he was harbouring more ambitious schemes. In 1505, with a view to enlarging his property, he bought an adjacent palace from the English College, and then subsequently acquired the adjoining house of his sister Giulia. Around 1515-1516, Julius II's policy of widening the streets adjacent to the palace opened up the possibility of a more direct link between Campo dei Fiori and the new Via Giulia. Alessandro decided to demolish the Palazzo Ferriz to make way for an ambitious architectural project designed by Antonio da Sangallo the Younger, who had been commissioned for the task from as early as 1514.

From the very outset it became apparent that the new palace would require a vastly extended amount of space. Thus, down till 1523, Cardinal Farnese systematically set about buying up adjacent property until he had acquired all of it. At the same time, in order to provide the palace with a fitting setting, Sangallo was commissioned to make radical alterations to the surrounding urban fabric. To open up the Via Baullari in

the direction of the Piazza Navona in exact alignment to the main entrance of the palace, he had dozens of houses demolished, and in front of the building laid out a huge square from where the entire façade was visible.

With the Sack of Rome in 1527, works ground to a halt. The cardinal's election to the papacy as Paul III in 1534 left him little time to pursue the project. Building resumed in 1541, on the basis of a new plan more befitting a papal residence drawn up by Sangallo, and was supervised by the new pope's son, Pier Luigi Farnese, then by his grandsons, continuing until well after the pontiff's death. In actual fact, the monumental task took more than sixty years to complete, marshalling the creative talents of some of the greatest of Renaissance architects. In 1546, Sangallo – who had been assisted by Jacopo Meleghino – died and was succeeded by Michelangelo, who was in turn followed by Vignola in 1555 and, finally, by Giacomo Della Porta in 1574. The death of Cardinal Alessandro Farnese in 1589 coincided with the official completion of building works on the palace.

Michelangelo is to be attributed with the completion of the façade by a grandiose cornice, the display of the Farnese grand coat of arms over the central first-storey window, and alterations to the courtyard designed by Sangallo: abandoning the projected superimposed arcades, he replaced them with windows surmounted by tympana – triangular on the first floor and semi-circular on the second – and two moulded garlands framing a bull's head, a typical Michelangelo motif borrowed from classical antiquity. The order is more monumental and gives the ensemble a more closed aspect.

The façade nevertheless retains the elegantly measured elevation intended by Sangallo, and its simplicity of line contrasts with the more ornamental character of Michelangelo's courtyard. Above the consoled ground-floor windows stand two perfectly symmetrical rows of windows: these feature no architectonic order but simply bring out, on the first storey, an alternating series of trangular and semi-circular tympana. The palace's massive imposing aspect, which strikes so many visitors when they reach the Piazza Farnese, was soon to be imitated by all Roman palazzi.

When, in 1550, Cardinal Ranuccio Farnese inherited the family residence, he commissioned the painter Francesco Salviati – succeeded, after his death in 1563, by the Zuccari brothers – with the decoration of the first-floor central room, the balcony of which stands over the grand entrance door.

Left hand page
The illusionistic ceiling of the famous Carracci Gallery revolutionised established pictorial schemes.

Above, top
The famous Carracci Gallery.

Above, bottom
The Room of the Labours of Hercules with, in the foreground, the colossal statue of the classical god excavated in Rome.

Previous pages (pp. 64-65)
The loggia of the façade looking out onto the gardens.

Top
Michelangelo's modified design for the interior courtyard.

Previous pages (pp. 68-69)
The Triumph of Bacchus, who holds a thyrsus and a bunch of grapes, accompanied by Ariane, and is led by a merry procession of bacchante musicians and the drunken figure of Silenus.

Above
The fine elevation of the Room of the Labours of Hercules, punctuated by antique busts and embellished with tapestries reproducing Raphael's Vatican frescoes.

Above, right
Framed by Annibale Carracci's astonishing trompe-l'œil *grisaille* herms, which perfectly imitate sculpture, Jupiter attempts to coax his wife Juno who is flanked by her traditional peacock.

The room – known as the Room of the Farnese Splendours – stylishly presents the epic of Farnese family ancestors since the 14th century, set against the lofty achievements of Paul III's pontificate. Ranuccio the Elder, a mercenary in the service of the papal armies, is the idolised forebear with whom his namesake, Cardinal Ranuccio, identifies and to whom an entire section of the north wall is dedicated: the massive silhouette of the warrior hero dominates the centre of the composition striking a pose inspired by that of Michelangelo's statue of Giuliano de' Medici in the San Lorenzo chapel in Florence.

On the death of Cardinal Alessandro Farnese, his nephew, Cardinal Odoardo Farnese, decided to continue the first-floor decoration works begun by his predecessors. Accordingly, in 1595, he summoned from Bologna – where their fame was at the time unrivalled – the brothers Annibale and Agostino Carracci, and commissioned them with the execution of the paintings in the grand gallery.

Owing to its ingenious design, Annibale's vaulted ceiling appears to be an extension of the wall surface; above the real cornice he added a second, illusionary cornice supported by painted imitation marble herms. In the openings thus created are a series of medallions, the green patina of which perfectly imitates bronze; these medallions alternate with large *quadri riportati*, their heavy gold frames apparently balancing on the ceiling cornice. The panels, portraying naked figures in often

Above
On the north wall in the Room
of Splendours, Salviati celebrates
the key events in the pontificate
of Paul III, enthroned in the centre
of the composition.

Opposite
On either side of this imposing
chimney-piece lie copies of allegorical
figures sculpted by Michelangelo
for Paul III's funerary monument.

comic postures, recount the unbridled amorous frolics of the Olympian gods and goddesses and represent a resounding celebration of triumphant Love.

The second floor still houses the extremely fine library built up over the centuries by the Farnese, even though most of the books were transferred to Naples in 1714, when the last of the line, Elisabetta Farnese, married a Bourbon of Naples. A similar fate befell the priceless collections of paintings, drawings and antiques from which artists had been freely allowed to draw inspiration. Some of these artists, such as El Greco, the Carracci brothers or the French sculptor Pierre Legros, had even been offered accommodation on the top floor of the palace.

On the death of Cardinal Odoardo in 1626, the palace ceased to be the Farnese residence, becoming instead the Roman embassy of the Duchies of Parma and Piacenza, and later that of the Kingdom of Naples. From then on, the palazzo was given over to stately receptions, continuously playing host to the most illustrious guests before finally, at the end of the 19th century, becoming the French embassy to the Italian Republic.

Opposite
The central arch
of the rear façade stands
in exact alignment
to the main entrance
of the palazzo.

Left
In a trompe-l'œil architectural setting
featuring *quadri riportati*, imitation
bronze medallions and *grisaille* herms,
the cyclops Polyphemus charms
Galatea with his flute.

The Palazzo Ricci-Sacchetti

Having worked as an architect at St Peter's, Antonio da Sangallo the Younger managed, in 1542, to acquire a plot on the Via Giulia from the basilica chapter in order to build a residence for his own family. Here he adopted a cubic design reminiscent of the Palazzo Farnese, laid out around a square courtyard onto which two loggias opened. The ground-floor windows of the façade, which rest on imposing consoles resembling bent knees, and the rusticated masonry highlighting the corners of the building and contrasting with the brick facing, provide an elegant display in a typically Sangallesque vein. On the ground-floor level of the building the traces of former arches can still be seen. Now walled up, they originally provided entrances to the shops opening onto the small adjacent street.

Sangallo's original design was on a smaller scale than the one adopted by the Ricci family in the late 16th century: the plans drawn up by the architect feature a two-storey building, with an additional attic storey and three rows of five windows each. The original façade was proudly embellished with the coat of arms of Paul III, Sangallo's homage to his papal patron. Following the architect's death in 1546, his son briefly inherited the palace before selling it to Cardinal Giovanni Ricci in 1552.

Above
A masked fountain adds a lively touch along the Via Giulia.

Left hand page
The charming Italian parterre at the Palazzo Ricci-Sacchetti, dotted with terracotta pots containing citrus fruit trees.

Below
This colossal female head guards
the grotto at the foot of the garden.

Ricci, who held the coveted post of secret treasurer to Julius III, as well as the office of majordomo to Cardinal Alessandro Farnese, aspired to a residence worthy of his rank. No sooner had he acquired the palace than he commissioned Francesco Salviati to begin an impressive programme of interior decoration. This brilliant pupil of Michelangelo's, who was also working on the Room of Splendours in the Palazzo Farnese, was the leading representative of a mannerist painting then highly fashionable in Rome at the time. On the high walls of the central room, known as the Globe Room because of the astonishing twin 16th-century globes which stand imposingly in the centre of the room, Salviati created a breathtaking pictorial ensemble, deploying a series of superimposed paintings, sculptures, architectonic settings and tapestries to produce illusionist effects in a refined fantastic style. He demonstrated his supreme mastery of pictorial technique in meticulous, highly elaborate compositions, depicting the story of Kind David with mannerist monumental figures much indebted to Michelangelo. The twin suites of four rooms leading off from the main room are embellished with friezes of painted panels framed by stucco figures, the work of the French painter and sculptor Ponce, who took over from Salviati in 1554-1555 while the latter was in France. The panels depict episodes from the Old Testament, the legend of Romulus and Remus founding the Eternal City, and the epic adventures of Ulysses.

Opposite
Sangallo paid particular attention
to the details on the façade
of his residence.

Above
The walled garden, with four
quadrangular parterres laid out around
a small fountain basin, has retained
the unassuming appearance
of the 16th-century humanist garden.

A few months later, in 1553, Cardinal Ricci acquired the house adjacent to the palace. Nanni di Baccio Bigio, who worked with Antonio da Sangallo and who, a few years later, was to draw up the plan of the Villa Medici for the same cardinal, was commissioned to carry out extension works. Accordingly, the original structure was extended on both sides; a sixth window was added to each storey, the main doorway was moved, and the central courtyard was widened. Cardinal Ricci continued to live in his palace up till his death in 1574. In a series of speculative transactions, he sold the property to his own nephew, bought it back, re-sold it to the Duke of Terranova then repurchased it once again, all the time remaining the sole tenant of the building.

In 1576, the Ricci family sold the palace to the Ceoli, newcomers in the influential Roman banking circles. Tiberio Ceoli carried out further extensions, adding a new storey to the building, as well two wings that faced the Tiber and enclosed a small walled garden. The rows of prophets and sibyls on the walls of the grand gallery, faithful copies of the pendentive figures adorning the ceiling of the Sistine Chapel, provide a further demonstration of the key influence of Michelangelo's mannerist style on late 16th-century painting. The proliferation of stucco ornamentation and the omnipresent gilding, both on the picture frames and the drapes of the *putti* which proudly bear the grand coat of arms of the Sacchetti, are indicative of the prevailing taste for elegantly mannered decoration.

Owing to financial difficulties, the antique statuary which formerly stood in the wall niches had to be sold off in the early 17th century to the Vatican archeological collections and was replaced by plaster copies. In 1608, Tiberio Ceoli sold the palace to Cardinal Aquaviva who, in turn, introduced a number of changes such as the building of a chapel over the courtyard loggia, whose dome and small lantern are typical of Pietro da Cortona, who is thought to have been the designer.

In 1649, the palace was definitively acquired by the Marquesses Sacchetti who have remained its fortunate proprietors down to this day. Virtually unchanged since then, the Palazzo Ricci-Sacchetti is still one of the finest architectural showpieces to be found along the sumptuous Via Giulia.

THE VILLA: MANNERIST INFLUENCES

The latter half of the 16th century witnessed the emergence of a more imaginative architectural style which cheerfully flouted the rigid tenets professed by Bramante and Raphael in imitation of classical antiquity. Mannerism adopted a medley of materials and styles: white marble statuary, polychrome veined-marble columns, stuccoed and gilded ceilings, wall frescoes, mosaics and shell-work in artificial garden grottos. Such features were blended into elegantly refined compositions which cultivated a taste for illusionism. The mannerist approach sought to create startling effects, using contrasting forms and complex compositions.

Following Michelangelo's highly ornate cornice at the Palazzo Farnese, sculpted decoration gradually invested Roman palazzi façades which were soon covered with lushly foliated Corinthian capitals, voluptuously shaped caryatids, convoluted cartouches and shell-work, grimacing masks, heraldic emblems, and friezes depicting chubby *putti* laden with heavy festoons. Architects sought to create pictorial effects by carefully arranging columns and pilasters and multiplying the contrasts between filled spaces and voids.

Vignola was the first architect to deliberately flout classical rules and the residence he designed for Pope Julius III on the slopes of the Parioli hills marked an important turning point in the evolution of villa architecture. Julius III enjoyed home comforts; he rarely strayed far from Rome, preferring to retire to the Villa Giulia, the sumptuous villa that bore his name, where he could relax, in the privacy of his personal nymphaeum, taking the waters to alleviate the suffering caused by his chronic gout.

Above
During the mannerist period, the stucco frames of paintings became increasingly ornate and featured grotesque motifs.

Opposite
The windows on the façade
of the Palazzo Madama are
embellished with exuberantly
contoured stucco frames.

Below, left
Stucco niches and decoration create
a contrast between voids and filled
spaces, multiplying the effects
of light and shadow on the marble
bodies of the statuary.

Below, right
The Villa Giulia nymphaeum offers
a fine illustration of mannerist delight
in mingling different materials: mosaic
work, marble, stone and stucco are
superimposed in infinite variations.

The Villa Giulia

In 1550, shortly after his unexpected election to the papacy, Cardinal Giovanni Maria Ciocchi del Monte – who assumed the title of Pope Julius III – began to take a closer interest in the *vigna* which he had inherited from his uncle and which stood on the upper slopes of the Parioli hills. Indeed, this villa, unlike the one he had initially planned to have built in his native region, offered all the advantages of proximity to Rome. In the years following his election, the new pope was content to enlarge and convert the old original residence.

Other lands, stretching across the Parioli hills to the north from the Via Flamina in the west, were soon added to the *vigna vecchia*: the *vigna del monte* on the upper slopes, the *vigna da basso* down in the valley and, finally, the *vigna del porto*, a small strip of land lying between the Via Flamina and the Tiber from which the pope could easily reach the Vatican by boats.

Before long, papal expenditure was channelled into building a new villa, designed as a veritable *casino* of delights, entirely given over to pontifical pleasure. It stood facing the Tiber valley, which itself would soon be renamed Giulia in honour of the papal residence. Work commenced in 1551 and was completed in record time. No fewer than three architects – Giorgio Vasari, Vignola and Bartolomeo Ammanati – took part in the project while a string of painters and stucco workers, including Prospero Fontana, Taddeo Zuccari and Federico Brandani, were involved in decorating the palace.

Previous pages (pp. 86-87)
The main façade of the Villa Giulia
enhanced by Vignola's central doorway
in rusticated masonry.

Above
The loggia of the first courtyard offers
a view down into the splendid
nymphaeum with its paving
and mosaic marine deities.

Top right hand page
The spring waters which fed the
nymphaeum and helped alleviate
Julius III's gout flow behind
the voluptuous caryatids.

Bottom right hand page
From the first-floor balcony, Pope
Julius III could freely contemplate
the Tiber valley which, for a time,
was named Giulia in his honour.

Although Giorgio Vasari was doubtless the first to have a hand in the design of the villa, following disagreements with the pope he was replaced by Vignola who had trained as a painter in Bologna and had only recently taken up architecture. The completed project may be attributed to the latter architect. He used it as a testing ground for his theories concerning the principles of classical architecture, theories which he was to publish a few years later in his *Rule of the Five Orders*, soon to become a standard reference work for all Renaissance architects.

At the Villa Giulia, he was commissioned with the construction of a hydraulic network to pipe water from the uphill Acqua Vergine spring down to the nymphaeum. The task of designing and decorating the main feature of the villa – the nymphaeum itself – the main feature of the villa – was entrusted to the sculptor Ammanati.

The plan of the villa combines two simple geometric figures which constantly occur: the square and the semi-circle. The apparently straightforward overall scheme, laid out on either side of a central axis, in fact conceals an interior of much greater complexity. Indeed, the main perspective is not immediately perceptible and the ensemble cannot be taken in at a single glance. The main building is an austere two-storeyed edifice, and the eye instantly focusses on the monumental arch of the central doorway, highlighted by rusticated masonry and flanked by two niches which are echoed on the upper storey. Set back on either side of this relatively shallow building, which had only three rooms per floor, are two large symmetrical wings accommodating staircases and bedrooms. The ceilings of the two ground-floor rooms, by Taddeo Zuccari, are embellished with depictions of divine banquets, processions of nymphs and other bacchic scenes, allusions to the lively social life of a villa entirely given over to epicurean pleasures. The friezes in the three first-floor bedrooms, painted by Prospero Fontana, alternately depict views of Rome or diverse mythological scenes, hence their poetic names: the "Chamber of the Seasons", the "Chamber of the Seven Hills" and the "Chamber of Arts and Sciences".

The vestibule leads to the rear façade which sweeps out onto the court via two long curving porticos provided with a series of elegant bays resting on slender columns boasting Ionic capitals. The portico ceiling is decorated with a mock bamboo-cane pergola on which are perched mischievous *putti* who throw flowers at the passing visitors... or urinate on their heads!

The central alley of a vast court, a hemicycle criss-crossed by parterres and formerly bordered by tall trees, runs down to the end wall where another echoing loggia stands with three arched bays. Like a classical triumphal arch, that loggia was formerly embellished with magnificent bas-reliefs and statues of Roman emperors from Julius III's extraordinary collection of antiquities. The three hundred statues, bas-reliefs, vases and bowls were not, as is normally the case, merely put on public display for æsthetic reasons, but formed an integral part of the building itself. The loggia acts as a huge open vestibule, artfully providing a link between the first and second courtyards. Its ribbed vault rests on small elegant polychrome

Centre
The parterres in the
garden adjacent
to the villa blend
in harmoniously with
the architecture
of the building.

Above
The loggia vault recreates
the rustic atmosphere
of a pergola with gaily
frolicking *putti*.

Opposite
The perspective from
the central doorway
is exactly aligned with
the loggia standing
at the foot of the first
courtyard.

marble-veined columns which seem to shimmer in the light of the setting sun.

Two curving flights of steps surround the hemicycle of the second courtyard and drop gently to a lower level which in turn encompasses the third, level of the nymphaeum itself. The semicircular outline of the nymphaeum space is bordered by a fine stone balustrade from where one can admire the splendid fan-shaped motif of the green and yellow marble-paved bed of the aquatic theatre. The paving stops short as the bed culminates in a smaller semicircle where the waters of the Acqua Vergine spring flow in. Four caryatids ceremonially stand guard over the precious waters which had such a tonic effect on the pontiff's gout; behind them, partially concealed, is the entrance to a maze of ambulatories formerly decorated

Above
A statue of a languid river god about to dispense fruit from his cornucopia.

Opposite
The elegant elevation of the loggia linking the first and second courtyards, framed by finely worked classical bas-reliefs.

with mythological frescoes and stucco work by Ammanati. At the end of the courtyard the wall opens skywards in an ethereal Serlian arched bay – so called in honour of the architect Sebastiano Serlio – offering a glimpse of the trees in the second garden. Today, the precious stucco facing composed of trophies and friezes of ivy, foliation and olive branches which ran along the pilasters, arches and cornice, has disappeared.

Julius III was apparently particularly fond of the nymphaeum courtyard where he would hold sumptuous banquets; and it was there, in early 1555, that he finally passed away, a victim of his chronic gout.

The villa was confiscated from the pope's heirs by the Apostolic Chamber who transferred practically all of the antiquities to the Vatican. In the 17th century, it became an official residence for high-ranking visitors, including Queen Christina of Sweden. Acquired by the Italian government in 1887, it is today home to the Etruscan Museum.

Above
Paintings by Ammanati depicting
the legends of Olympian gods
and goddesses on the vaulted ceiling
of this recently restored room.

Opposite
Bas-reliefs from Julius III's collection
of antiquities blend harmoniously
into the architectural structure
of the building.

Above
Satyrs and *putti* gaily fight over
bunches of grapes on the loggia trellis.

The Sacro Bosco, Bomarzo

The unorthodox use of the caryatids as guardian figures symbolised the poetically playful vein in which the Villa Giulia nymphaeum had been designed. During the same period, that vein was to be exploited to the full in a park in the vicinity of Rome designed as a resounding hymn to the forces of Nature.

It was to escape from the narrow confines of Roman social life, or perhaps from his wife, the young Giulia Farnese whose affair with the scandalous Borgia Pope Alexander VI was public knowledge in Roman aristocratic circles, that Prince Vicino Orsini, scion of one of the most venerable Roman families, designed the highly eccentric garden at Bomarzo, his ancestral homeland, not far from Viterbo.

"To soothe his heart", as he was to put it himself, the prince devoted thirty years of his life to laying out this strange garden, tucked away in the depths of a picturesque valley between outcrops of tufa rock and Etruscan tombs. There, amidst the oak and chestnut trees, he laid out alleys lined with startling gigantic stone sculptures of monstrous figures which rise up out of the rocky landscape. This fantastic bestiary formed a poetic literary garden, a reflection of Prince Orsini's own cultivated personality.

An unsuccessful courtier, the prince found solace in the contemplation of wild nature where, to his mind, all notion of social rank was at last banished. In the company of literary

Above
The paths through the wood are lined with giant animals and fabulous creatures.

Left hand page
The leaning Sacro Bosco tower, deliberately built askew, exemplifies Prince Orsini's non-conformist spirit.

Above
This small classically-inspired temple
was erected to the memory of the fair
Giulia Farnese, Prince Orsini's fickle
wife.

Opposite
In the middle of a clearing bordered
by a small wall bristling with pine cones,
a stone bear presents the Orsini coat
of arms to visitors.

friends such as the poet Annibale Caro, he wandered, like Ariosto's *Orlando Furioso*, in search of his beloved, engaging in imaginary combat with the legendary creatures which crossed his path. Enthralled by the tales of voyagers who had set foot in the New World, Prince Orsini had exotic plants sent back from those mysterious lands to be cultivated in his garden. An initiatory and allegorical journey, the sacred wood of Bomarzo in a way represents the antithesis of the Renaissance garden.

Laid out over an area of more than seven acres on rugged terrain that rises and falls over a hundred feet, the garden hugs the contours of the landscape, and visitors are continously obliged to clamber up and down its winding paths. Beyond a small bridge spanning a rushing torrent, the entrance to the park is signalled by a curious mediaeval arch. From there on, visitors, in the absence of all guidance as to which route to follow, are left entirely to their own devices. The garden marks a definitive break with the cherished rules of symmetry and perspective found in Renaissance villas. A few geometrically designed spaces offer some respite: the Theatre of Love, with the Grotto of Venus at the end of the exedra, on the lowest level of the wood; the rectangular clearing lined by huge urns of Etruscan inspiration which marks the intermediate level; and the vast, grassy hippodrome at the top of the hill, which is crowned by a classically-inspired temple. Apart from these open spaces, visitors are obliged to stumble blindly through the wood, crossing paths bristling with tortoises, dragons, Cerberus watchdogs, elephants, harpies, ogres and other strange monsters which lurk in its depths.

Right from its completion in 1552, the Bomarzo Wood disconcerted contemporary visitors. They looked askance at its winding paths and the somewhat disturbing nature of its stone monsters which seemed to betray all too well the solitary tortured mind of the prince. The place lacked any overall plan of organisation and flouted the immutable reassuring laws of symmetry. Scoffed at and scorned, the wood sank into utter oblivion following the death of the prince in 1584 and remained in that sorry state despite attempts made to revive its fortunes by the Lante della Rovere family who acquired it in the 17th century. In the aftermath of World War II, it was Salvador Dali, the leading light of Surrealism who, captivated by the futuristic extravagance of the sculptures and the wild abandoned aspect of the place, drew attention to its plight. Not long afterwards, the Bettini family acquired the property. Enchanted by its sylvan monsters, they carefully nursed it back to life and its magic treasures are today once more open to public visit.

Above
This fearsome monster must have made many a visitor shudder.

Top left hand page
From the top of his rocky promontory, the god Neptune seems to preside over the mysteries of the wood.

Bottom left hand page
A slumbering nymph awaits the Prince Charming who will awaken her from her dreams...

THE GOLDEN AGE OF THE ROMAN VILLA

Paul IV was the antithesis of his predecessor Julius III. An austere, solitary pope, and a proud Neapolitan, his fervent piety led him to eschew earthly temptations and to seek peace in isolation. He was a founder of the Theatine Order, and his preferred lifestyle was closely akin to the monastic ideal. During the summer months, he would retire to the Theatine monastery of San Silvestro al Quirinale, accompanied only by three or four chamberlains and his guards. Towards the end of his life, he became increasingly disinterested in the political affairs of the papacy which he left in the hands of his nephew, Cardinal Carlo Carafa, and fleeing the bustle of the Vatican, he moved to the more peaceful Villa Belvedere. Even here, life seemed too hectic to his taste and so he commissioned a little *casino* – provided with no more than a loggia, a fountain and a few bedrooms – to be built in the Vatican woods. The project was shelved on his death and was only completed under Pius IV who, for his part, envisaged a totally different use for the building, adapting it to much more hedonistic purposes...

From the very outset of his cardinalship, Pius IV had proved to be extremely partial to the pleasures of vacation. He was a tireless traveller, frequently changing residences. The *avvisi*, those indispensible courriers who, in the Italy of the day, would be dispatched to their masters by intelligence agents in the service of great men, were hard put to keep up with a pontiff ever on the move. Pius IV assiduously frequented all the residences placed at his disposal – the Venetian Palace, Cardinal d'Este's *vigna* on the Quirinale and the Villa Belvedere in Rome, charming Ostia, Frascati, Tivoli and La Magliana – often moving on to a new place every day or trying out all the bedrooms available at any one stopping place!

When Pius V succeeded to the papal throne, the court found itself once more plunged into a climate of austerity, scarcely amenable to the enjoyment of the easy life. The new pope, who had been appointed Inquisitor General by Paul IV, was more noted for his monastic lifestyle – a legacy of his Dominican training – than for any propensity for enjoying earthly pleasures. Accordingly, he cleared the immodest pagan statuary that had so delighted his predecessor out of the Villa Belvedere, and removed all the seats so that the

Top
The view down to the parterres at the Villa Lante, with fountains laid out along the main alley running across the wooded hillside.

Bottom
The Organ Fountain with its mighty jets of water dominates the ponds along the esplanade at the Villa d'Este.

traditional plays could no longer be performed there. The papal court was forced to swelter in the intolerable Roman heat during the summer months as the pope himself was content to remain cloistered in the Vatican to the utter despair of his entourage. Pius V considered that the cardinals' fondness for increasingly luxurious vacation retreats was in total contradiction to any religious ideal, and he exhorted them to lead lives more in keeping with the Holy Scriptures.

Such policies, however, did not put a halt to the fashion for spending the summer away from the city, nor did they prevent summer residences from becoming ever more splendid. Vignola, in his various architectural projects, proved himself eminently capable of adapting to all situations and of providing the ideal response both to his clients' demands and to the constraints of the site. His spatial approach, combining both building and gardens, adopted at the Orti Farnesiani, the Palazzo Farnese at Caprarola, or the Villa Lante at Bagnaia, and which featured a succession of terraces linked by a cascade of balustraded stairs and crossed by a principal axis in direct alignment with the palace, was to have a profound influence on the gardens of Latium from the late 17th century onwards.

It was also Vignola, along with his rival, the architect and antiquary Pirro Ligorio, who explored the myriad possibilities offered by water in the gardens, building free-falling cascades and water-courses channelled down stone ramps, and constructing every imaginable type of fountain, quietly lining garden paths, or bristling with statues and musical hydraulic mechanisms. Pirro Ligorio achieved fame with the laying-out of the Villa d'Este; its terraced gardens and symmetrical alleys leading to breathtaking fountains were soon the talk of all Europe.

The Villa d'Este

In the early 16th century, the site on which Cardinal Ippolito II d'Este was to build his splendid residence was still occupied by a small Franciscan convent. Disappointed that he had not been elected by his peers to the throne of St Peter because of his extravagant social life and his pro-French leanings, Cardinal d'Este decided to retire to peaceful Tivoli and live the life of a veritable king. A lover of art and antiquities, extremely well-read and having long frequented the French royal court, Cardinal d'Este may be regarded as one of the most refined and cultivated men of his day. His relationship with Pirro Ligorio, into whose expert hands he straight away entrusted the site acquired in 1550, was characterised by perfect mutual understanding.

That historian, antiquary, architect and occasional painter, who played a prominent role in Roman cultural circles in the latter half of the 16th century, was to offer his client a skilfully designed ensemble based on the mythical model of the Garden of the Hesperides. In the centre of the garden, in homage to the cardinal, he erected a statue of Hercules, the hero who managed to take possession of the precious golden apples. Ligorio was to be decisively influenced by excavations being undertaken at the time at the nearby Villa Hadriana, carefully analysing its various component features, such as theatre, exedra, basins, and fountains and closely studying the manner in which they were integrated into the surrounding landscape. In an ultimate touch of illusionism, antique pieces,

dug out of the subsoil, were even to be displayed in the gardens at the Villa d'Este.

The gardens, which to the north hug the slopes of the Alban hills, are abruptly cut off from the valley in the northwest by a sheer cliff. Massive earthworks were undertaken on the steep terrain in order to lay out vast terraces linked by wide staircases, offering sublime panoramic views out onto the Roman campagna. The gardens are criss-crossed by numerous, wide, oak-bordered alleys dissecting the central axis that runs straight from the villa entrance.

The gardens were formerly entered from the lower terrace and not, as is the case today, from the villa located at the top of the hill. Visitors reached the monumental north-west entrance, framed by two fountains, by a minor road which branched off from the Via Tibur, the ancient Roman highway running between the city and Tivoli. This entrance led onto a vast esplanade divided by two perpendicular alleys covered with pergolas of vines and jasmine, and framed on either side by four rigorously quadrilateral mazes of myrtle hedge. That first section, planted with aromatic herbs and flowers, was embellished with small pavilions. One of the pergola-covered alleys led to a second terrace with four large fishponds, formerly bordered by vases with fountain jets. On the left, two steep alleys climbed up to a fabulous hydraulic organ operated by a water-powered mechanism which produced musical sounds.

Previous pages (pp. 104-105)
From the overhanging terrace crossed by a small stream symbolising the Tiber and featuring the Rometta Fountain with its miniature theatre, the view takes in the entire valley below.

Left hand page
In the villa gardens, acquatic displays are provided in every imaginable form: basins, waterfalls, gushing fountains, and clouds of fine spray.

Opposite
On top of the dome surmounting the Hydraulic Organ Fountain, Victory presides over the glorious destiny of the Villa d'Este.

Above
The bizarre masks along the Alley of the Hundred Fountains contribute to the fantastic atmosphere which inspired the poet Gabriele d'Annunzio.

Amidst the murmur of the fountains, three parallel staircases cross over to a small copse skirting the oval basin of the Dragon Fountain, where a many-headed monster spouts its powerful jet of water skywards, and come out on the famous Alley of the Hundred Fountains. The alley, which stretches out for more than a hundred and fifty yards, features a procession of stone sculptures – eagles (the emblem of the Este), lilies (the emblem of the King of France) and barques (the emblem of the Church) – all spouting countless jets of water which then collects and flows out of chimera heads into a second channel a few feet below. The visitor may turn left towards the Tivoli Fountain, a huge semicircular basin enclosed by an arcaded exedra wall covered in ferns, in the middle of which roaring water overflows from a massive bowl, or right, towards the Rometta, a veritable miniature theatre filled with scale models of the most outstanding buildings of Ancient Rome of which today mere vestiges remain. Transverse alleys run through the final, steeper section of the gardens up to the last terrace where the villa stands.

Nowadays, visitors enter the gardens from the villa. From a back street in the town of Tivoli, a small side door leads into the courtyard around which the villa is laid out. Visitors pass through suites of rooms, still decorated with somewhat faded frescoes, the products of a nobler age, and, emerging into the brilliant sunlight onto the terrace in front of the villa's rear façade, are confronted by the immense gardens.

The villa's innumerable fountains were fed by an aqueduct which piped one hundred gallons of water per second from the River Aniente. As soon as they were opened, the gardens became a hugely popular attraction, reproduced in countless contemporary engravings. Their celebrity spread beyond the frontiers of Italy to all Europe, from the court of Emperor Maximilian in Vienna to that of Queen Catherine de Medici in Paris. Ambassadors, scientists, artists – such as the French painters Fragonard and Hubert Robert – and writers, such as Montaigne, flocked to the Villa d'Este to behold with their own eyes the fabulous spectacle.

On the cardinal's death in 1572, the villa was briefly taken over by the Apostolic Chamber. Restored to the Este family, the gardens were completed by Cardinal Alessandro d'Este in 1624 and, throughout the 17th century, new fountains, such as the Bicchierone Fountain by Pietro and Gian Lorenzo Bernini, were added.

Top
Framed by twin caryatids whose legs culminate in a corkscrewing spiral, this bas-relief on the Organ Fountain depicts the musical duel between Apollo and Pan.

Bottom
The Grotto of Diana features an excessive display of juxtaposed shingle, mosaic work and pumice stone, typical of Renaissance nymphaeums.

Below
On the ceiling of the central first-floor
room, merrily feasting Olympian deities
celebrate the wedding of Eros
and Psyche.

Above
Enigmatic stone sphinxes embellish
the staircase parapets.

Opposite
A pathway, streaming with water, runs
behind the moss-covered arcades of the
Oval Fountain and its cascading overflow.

Below
An allegorical representation of bountiful,
many-breasted Nature dispensing earthly blessings
to mankind.

Towards the end of the 18th century, following the marriage of the Este heir to the Archduke of Austria, the villa was acquired by the Hapsburgs, who left it to languish in a state of neglect. Between 1850 and 1896, its fortunes were revived when it was rented to Cardinal Gustave de Hohenlohe who carried out necessary repairs, and planted palm trees, sequoias and Lebanese cedars. Famous artists, including Franz Liszt, who dedicated two piano pieces to the villa gardens, were received with great ceremony. Today, the gardens belong to the Italian State and continue to delight countless visitors.

Above
A mock fountain in mosaic and shingle work, similar to those embellishing the villa gardens, stands in the centre of the first-floor room with frescoes painted by the Zuccari brothers.

Opposite
The massive shell of the moss-covered Bicchierone Fountain, attributed to Bernini, stands on the axis of the tiered terraces overlooking the gardens.

Above
In the Alley of the Hundred
Fountains, myriad fountain jets
spout from the mouths
of grotesque masks and from
lichen-covered eagles, lilies
and barques.

The Palazzo Farnese

In the opening years of the 16th century, Cardinal Alessandro Farnese, the future Pope Paul III, was appointed perpetual vicar of Ronciglione, a village south of Viterbo, and bought the nearby lands of Caprarola from Francesco Maria della Rovere. His ambition was to establish a vast *signoria* stretching from Ronciglione northwards to the lands inherited from his family around Lake Bolsena, in order to provide a solid foothold for the Farnese who were assuming an increasingly important role in Roman society. At the time, Italy was still riven by bloody internecine rivalries, so the cardinal decided to turn Caprarola into a family stronghold and, between 1515 and 1520, commissioned Antonio da Sangallo the Younger to build a fortress on the highest point in the village.

Work ground to a halt in 1534, however, when Cardinal Farnese, newly elected pope, was confronted with other more pressing preoccupations. Following his death, it was his grandson, the second Cardinal Alessandro Farnese, who re-instigated work on the site in the years 1556-1558. Meanwhile, the Farnese position had been strengthened thanks to the nepatism on of Paul III and the family dukedom was now firmly implanted around the town of Castro. Sangallo's original military project was thus transformed into a summer residence, more in tune with the new mood of the time.

Above
One of the two surviving gardens
flanking the rear of the palace.

Previous pages (pp. 114-115)
The grandiose theatrical setting
designed by Vignola at Caprarola.

Overleaf (p. 115), right
The houses of the village and,
beyond, the Farnese domains seen
from the first-floor balcony.

Opposite
Overlooking the parterres
of the *palazzina*, this parapet,
embellished with stone dolphins,
leads to the rear terrace.

Top, right hand page
The fountain in the Room
of the Labours of Hercules depicts
a view of Rome.

Centre, right hand page
River god at the top of the stone
ramp leading to the *palazzina*.

Bottom, right hand page
A rose pergola, a traditional feature
of the Italian garden.

The feudal nature of the original scheme was nevertheless still apparent in the revised project submitted by Vignola, the architect chosen by the Farnese. In his spectacularly theatrical design, the new building, perched on its rocky spur, towers over the village of Caprarola, and visitors climbing up to the palace from the main street immediately experience the sensation of being crushed by its imposing mass. At Cardinal Farnese's request, Vignola completely altered the layout of the town, and introduced a main axis which ran from the central doorway of the palace and split the town down the middle. Houses were aligned on either side of that axis according to the social class of the occupants, those belonging to local worthies being located closest to the palace.

On reaching the top of the main street by coach or on horseback, visitors then rode up a curved ramp to a vast esplanade. From there, they had to proceed on foot up two straight flights of stairs to a second terrace, the threshold of the cardinal's residence, from where they could admire the village below and the surrounding horizon at their leisure. Arriving in such a manner, even the highest-ranking cardinal could not fail to be impressed.

Vignola kept the foundations of the fortress that Sangallo had designed, and its bastions surrounded by deep ditches together with the rusticated facing work of the lower part of the building lent the new palace a decidedly military air. Of the original drawbridges which allowed access to the building across moats, only those leading to the gardens at the rear have survived. The pentagonal plan that Sangallo had conceived was also retained by Vignola.

It was Vignola, however, who was responsible for the novel distribution of the rooms, according to their function as private or public space. All the large state rooms (the Room of the Labours of Hercules, the Room of Splendours and the Map Room) are located at the front of the building and have direct access to the loggia of the grand interior circular courtyard. Conversely, the smaller private rooms – the cardinal's summer and winter apartments – are relegated to the rear of the building. The façade corresponds to a much more typical late Renaissance spirit, featuring rhythmical rows of elegant pilasters with Corinthian capitals, while large arched first-storey windows, topped by a cluster of small windows on the storey above, provide ample openings to the exterior.

An extraordinary spiral staircase leads up from the Guards Room on the ground floor. Designed by Vignola, it is known

FRANCISCVS·GALLIA...
COMPRIMENDAE·DEFECTI...
ET·ALEXANDRVM·
DE·REBVS·LEG...
AMPLISSIMO·APPARAT...

118

The two Zuccari brothers and their father are portrayed bearing the canopy which shelters the French King François I, the German Emperor Charles V and Cardinal Alessandro Farnese in this scene from *The Entry to Paris* (1540) on the walls of the Room of Splendours.

Above, and right hand page
The spectacular sweep of the twin-columned Scala Regia, punctuated by Farnese lilies.

as the Scala Regia in reference to Bramante's staircase at the Vatican and is supported on sets of twin columns. It features an architrave carved with lilies, the heraldic emblem of the Farnese and sweeps up majestically to a fresco-painted loggia which girdles the grand circular open courtyard.

A first door on the right leads into the Room of the Labours of Hercules, bathed in the soft light from large glazed arcades. The first-floor balcony in the centre of the façade offers a panoramic view out over the surrounding Farnese domains, while on the walls inside the visitor is confronted by painted views depicting – like so many trophies – other towns belonging to the family which lie beyond the horizon.

Beyond this first state room is a small round chapel decorated with Old Testament scenes, followed by a second state room, known as the Room of the Farnese Splendours. The vaulted ceiling, as in the similar room at the Palazzo Farnese in Rome, depicts the lofty achievements of family ancestors, while the walls proudly commemorate notable political events from the pontificate of Paul III. In these historical scenes, which are veritable family photographs and feature various major protagonists of the day such as the French King François I and the German Emperor Charles V – Cardinal Alessandro Farnese ensured that he was portrayed in the foreground alongside his grandfather the pope. The frescoes, painted by the brothers Taddeo and Federico Zuccari, who were in overall charge of the decoration works, set out what is in effect political programme, drawn up by the cardinal so as to present himself as the worthy successor of Paul III to the papal throne.

The visitor continues through other rooms, each featuring a particular iconographical theme, usually related to the cardinal's own virtues, and passes through the splendid Map Room – with its vaulted ceiling depicting the planetary system and its walls displaying maps of the entire known world such as it was in the late 16th century – before at last reaching the gardens proper at the rear of the villa. Shaded paths, breaking with the symmetry of orthodox Renaissance gardens, take him to the small summer pavilion which the cardinal had built in the most secluded corner of the garden. Two symmetrical flights of steps on either side of the stone ramp, embellished with dolphins and down which flows the water from the spring uphill, lead past the guardian figures of two bearded river gods holding cornucopia before reaching the vast esplanade in front

Above
Displayed on the walls of the
Map Room, the cartography
of the four continents as known
to the 16th century.

Opposite
Mysterious canephorae
representing the five senses
watch over the rigorously aligned
parterres of the *palazzina*.

of the *palazzina*. On either side of the small *casino* stretch
Italian parterres laid out around fountains with sculpted uni-
corns, symbols of purity and the family mascot of the Farnese.
Astonishing stone canephorae, each holding a finger to its lips
as if motioning visitors to remain silent, add to the enchanted
atmosphere.

Unfortunately, this peaceful spot is now closed to the
public, as the small pavilion is today the private property of the
Presidency of the Italian Republic.

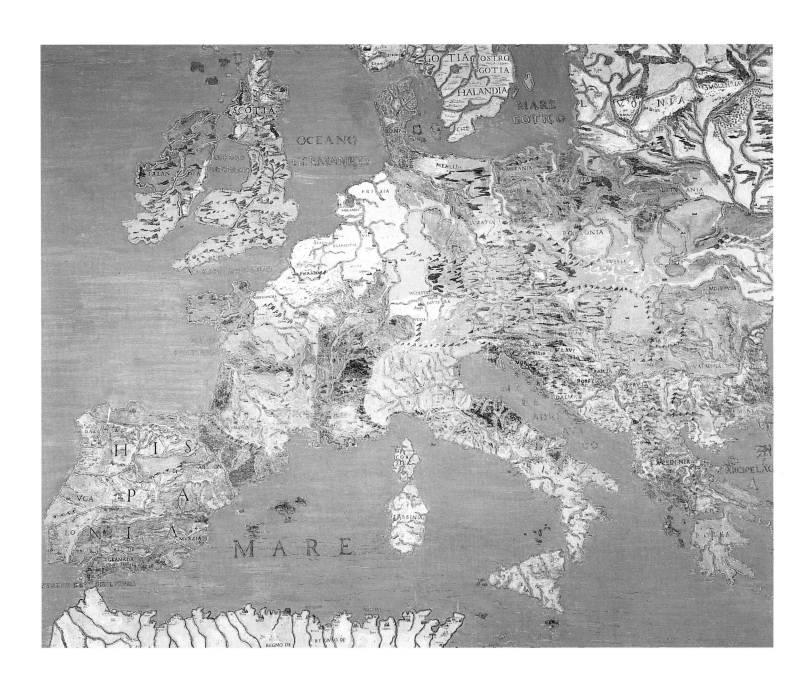

Above
A Europe in which Scandinavia
was peopled by Ostrogoths
and in which Scotland was still
an independent kingdom...

Opposite
On the vaulted ceiling of the Map
Room, zodiacal signs and planets
form a celestial map.

The Villa Lante

It was during the austere pontificate of Pius V that Cardinal Giovan Francesco Gambara, who had been appointed bishop of Viterbo, decided to build a sumptuous country residence in the vicinity of his bishopric, at Bagnaia, in order to rival Cardinal Alessandro Farnese's palace at Caprarola. The site was occupied by the game reserve which Cardinal Raffaele Riario had laid out in the early 16th century and where the court of Leo X had so often disported themselves. The passion for hunting, however, was by now on the wane and, in 1568, the highly cultivated and extremely ambitious young prelate asked Vignola, the architect of Caprarola, to build him a residence fit to impress the entire papal court.

In the villa's enclosure wall a central arch, dominated by a triangular pediment, offers a spectacular view onto the impeccably laid-out parterres of the gardens with, in the background on either side of the principal axis, the two pavilions behind which a long stone ramp climbs up the wooded hillside. Beyond, the view disappears into the trees. The plan of the villa is integrated into the slope of the hill, and has five different levels linked by stairways. The wild natural environment found in the shaded upper zone presents a stark contrast to the disciplined geometry of the lower zone. The villa itself consists of two separate *casini*, commanding an unbroken panoramic view over the gardens, the key feature of the ensemble.

Nowadays, access to the gardens is via a side entrance door alongside the Pegasus Fountain, a large circular basin, in the middle of which rears the bronze statue of the winged horse surrounded by four *bambini* blowing water from conches. The choice of Pegasus, the winged horse who accompanied the Muses, is a striking memorial to the cardinal's role as patron of the arts. Skirting the basin are two alleys: the alley on the left climbs up to the villa entrance, while that on the right leads off into the woods planted with holm oak and chestnut trees that are centuries old. Formerly, the route took visitors past fountains and sculptures symbolising the vicissitudes of human destiny from the lost Golden Age through the growing decadence of the Ages of Silver, Iron and Bronze.

A second transversal alley runs back to the villa gardens, enclosed behind high walls. The acquatic itinerary starts at the top of the hill where the spring gushes out of the rustic Grotto of the Flood, symbolising the end of the Golden Age. On either side, shaded by tall plane trees, stand twin pavilions dedicated to the Muses, from where the waters of the flood gush down onto the surprised visitor. On their façades is stamped the emblem of the crayfish – in Italian, *gambero* – which featured on Cardinal Gambara's coat of arms. The spring water pours into the octagonal Fountain of the Dolphins and runs off into the Crayfish Chain, a long ramp lined by yet more sculpted crayfish.

From there, the stream flows into the Fountain of the Giants, a circular basin flanked by two bearded river gods, symbolising the Arno and the Tiber, before being channelled across a long banqueting table, cooling the drinks as it passed; it then proceeds to the Fountain of the Snails where it gushes forth in a thousand jets before vanishing underground, finally to re-emerge amidst the lower parterres in the Fountain of the Moors where four sculpted ephebes graciously bear the coat of arms of Cardinal Montalto – five mountains surmounted by a star. This fountain stands in the centre of a small island joined by four small bridges which span the large quadrangular basin.

The natural element, water, is tamed by man, and its multiple resources exploited in ingenious ways; surrounded by statues, pavilions, basins and ramps in peperino stone, and rows of box hedges, the eye is constantly enchanted by thundering cascades, powerful jets, flowing streams and fine spray. However, it is the lower section of the gardens which offers the

Above
The spring water streams down
the Crayfish Chain to the final basin
in the series – the Fountain of the Moors
standing in the parterre, aligned
with the entrance arch.

Opposite
Marking the end of the wood,
one of the two pavilions bearing
the cardinal's symbolic crayfish emblem.

Previous pages (pp. 124-125)
The French-style serpentine scrolls
of the parterres at the Villa Lante.

Previous pages (pp. 128-129)
The impeccable layout of the Italian parterre
around the Fountain of the Moors.

Opposite, and bottom right hand page
The Pegasus Fountain below
the two pavilions at the Villa Lante.

Below
On the ceiling of one of the first-floor rooms,
stucco statuary and allegorical scenes prefigure
the splendours of the Baroque.

Top left, right hand page
The far wall of this ground-floor loggia
in one of the pavilions is embellished with
a painted view of the villa.

Top right, right hand page
The Fountain of the Giants framed
by two river deities: Tiber and Arno.

most marvelous display of human ingenuity: here, the box hedges between the two pavilions are arranged in winding scrolls to form the pontifical coat of arms; elsewhere, they coil round the Fountain of the Moors, laid out alternately in the traditional geometric compositions of the Italian parterre, or in the typically undulating style of the *jardin à la française*, the vogue for which was introduced in the 17th century by Louise Angélique de La Trémoille, wife of Duke Antonio Lante.

Montaigne, passing through Bagnaia, went into raptures over the beauty of the villa gardens which, to his mind, surpassed Tivoli by their sheer magnificence. Apparently the sole person to remain unimpressed by the splendours of the villa was the austere Cardinal Carlo Borromeo who dismissed them in the following terse condemnation: "Your Grace, the money you have squandered building this place would have been better spent on a convent for nuns" – words which reveal the prevalent frame of mind in a papal Rome dominated by the Jesuits. The warning must have achieved its desired effect: Cardinal Gambara immediately called a halt to the works, and it was left to Cardinal Alessandro Peretti Montalto, nephew of Sixtus V, to carry Vignola's project to completion.

On Montalto's death, in 1623, the villa was acquired by the Church which rented it out to various cardinals as an attractive summer retreat. In the latter half of the 17th century, Alexander VII granted the villa to the Lante family who remained in ownership until 1953, when they were obliged to hand it over to the Italian State.

Above
From the *bosco* terrace, a view
of the showcase façade of the Villa
Medici, studded with antique pieces
from the family collections.

Right hand page
The villa enclosure, criss-crossed
by garden parterres and pergola-
covered alleys, painted on the vaulted
ceiling of Ferdinand I de' Medici's
studiolo.

The Villa Medici

In 1564, on the site of the former Roman villa of Lucullus, famed for his epicurean lifestyle, Cardinal Giovanni Ricci, thanks to his influential Vatican post as secret treasurer to Julius III, acquired a plot of land on the Roman heights, just inside the Aurelian Wall. Although uncultivated, the plot commanded a magnificent panoramic view. Nanni di Baccio Bigio, designer of the Ricci palace in the Via Giulia, was commissioned with alteration works to the former Crescenzi *vigna*. While the original north section of the building was incorporated into the project, a twin-storeyed central section boasting two large salons on each floor was erected on the new espalanade on the garden side. These works entailed the demolition of two floors on the rear façade of the villa which was provided with an attractive loggia leading into the gardens. The land stretching to the Aurelian Wall, which enclosed the property on the north side, was laid out with sixteen box-hedge parterres.

On the death of Giovanni Ricci in 1574, the villa passed into the hands of an ambitious young cardinal, Ferdinand de' Medici, soon to be made Grand Duke of Tuscany. As Ferdinand doubtless felt that the Villa Ricci was not sufficiently majestic accommodation for a descendant of the Medici, the family architect, Bartolomeo Ammanati, was commissioned to carry out a series of alterations to the existing structure. Accordingly, the loggia of the rear façade was re-designed as a huge, tall Serliana surmounted by the Medici coat of arms with its six balls. The reception floor has three state rooms. On

Above
A sketch by F.-M. Granet
of the front façade of the
Villa Medici, seen behind
the twin towers of Trinità
dei Monte church
overlooking the steps
of the Piazza di Spagna.

Opposite
Beyond the parterre
with the Fountain
of the Obelisk can
be seen the arcades
of the terrace leading
to the *bosco*.

134

the ceiling of the Chamber of the Muses, the cardinal had painted his astrological birth chart which had accurately predicted that he would become Grand Duke of Tuscany despite the fact that, as fifth-born son of Cosimo I, any likelihood of this happening must have appeared extremely slim at the time. The paintings by Jacopo Zucchi in the ceiling coffers alternately depict allegories of the Muses and of planetary and zodiacal signs in an immense talisman designed to boost the cardinal's chances – although he did not hesitate to poison his sister-in-law in order to ensure that the prophecy was fulfilled! On the ground floor, the vestibule was enlarged to form a monumental entrance from whence a large central flight of steps, soon divided into two symmetrical sections, gave access to two spiral staircases – located at either end of the building – leading to the loggias and the upper floors. A perpendicular wing – a long gallery intended to house Cardinal de' Medici's collection of antiquities – was added to the main section of the building.

At the southern tip of the property, Ammanati opened an imposing rusticated doorway onto the Via di Porta Pinciana; from here, parallel to the main building, he laid out an alley almost half a mile long, lined by high walls, which ran to the esplanade in front of the villa. Visitors, whether they arrived by coach along this alley from the Porta Pinciana or via the ramp which climbed from the Piazza di Spagna, remained unaware of the villa's rear façade until they reached the esplanade where they discovered, to their astonishment, the immense theatrical decor covered with the priceless antique bas-reliefs, statuary and busts that made up the cardinal's collection, the future nucleus of the Uffizi Museum in Florence.

The entire façade is designed as a showcase intended to highlight the finest pieces in the collection: the virtually blind wall has hardly any openings but is filled instead, with a series of frames and niches, meticulously arranged in alternating symmetry, which house the precious objects. The impression of ostentation is alleviated by the vertical line of the twin belvedere towers which rise on either side of the main building and frame the roof garden. Beneath the bays of the central loggia, a pair of massive lions glare menacingly at Giambologna's graceful, sensual statue of Mercury, who seems poised to leap out of the fountain bowl.

Above
In the garden paths, voluptuous statues of the goddess Venus housed in a fountain niche or in a pavilion boasting a Serlian arch.

In the gardens, each bend in the paths, each little square offered the spectacle of antique statues, busts, bas-reliefs, obelisks or sarcophagi used as fountains or veritable open-air stage

sets. The walk through the parterres also held further somewhat different surprises as the visitor came across lions, tigers, bears, an ostrich or some of the other exotic beasts which haunted the place.

Not far from the Venus loggia stands the entrance to the second pavilion which Cardinal de' Medici had built at the foot of the garden. Rather than a *studiolo* (or study), as it is known today, it would seem that this pavilion, discreetly linked to the outside by stairs leading to the foot of the tower on the Aurelian Wall, was used by the cardinal as a *garçonnière* where he no doubt pursued studies of an altogether different nature...

Over the perpendicular wing, the cardinal had a huge belvedere-terrace built, from where, in the company of his guests, he could admire the view overlooking the elegant façade and garden parterres as well as the lush green countryside stretching away beyond the Aurelian Wall where, a few decades later, Cardinal Scipione Borghese was to build his own villa.

The terrace, sunlit throughout the day, leads to the refreshing shade of the *bosco*, a vast wooded zone above the gardens where one can seek privacy amidst the tall trees, seated on one of the small stone benches scattered along the paths. The main alley leads to the artificial hill built in the late 16th century on the ruins of the former Roman Temple of Fortune. After climbing the seemingly endless moss-covered steps up the slope, the visitor reaches a little belvedere at the summit, which commands a breathtaking panoramic view of Rome.

On the death of Ferdinand de' Medici, his son Charles lost interest in the property, preferring Florence to Rome. The 17th century proved a disastrous period for the villa and its

Above
On the ceiling in the Room of the Muses, the celestial muses designate the astrological birth chart of the cardinal, destined to become Grand Duke of Tuscany.

Opposite
Capricorn, emblem of Cardinal Ferdinand de' Medici.

Right hand page
Overrun with delightful grotesques, the vestibule leading to the cardinal's *garçonnière*.

misfortunes continued right through the following century when a large portion of its antiquities collections were transferred to the Medici museum in Florence.

Put up for sale by the Lorraine family who systematically depleted the Medici possessions, the villa was acquired in 1804 by the French government in exchange for the Palazzo Mancini in Via del Corso which had, up till then, accommodated the scholars – painters, sculptors and architects – of the French Academy in Rome.

Judging that the villa's peaceful surroundings offered ideal working conditions, the Academy took over the abandoned property and built studios and accommodation for the visiting artists. Finally, in the 1960s, under the supervision of the painter Balthus, restoration works were carried out on the frescoes in the apartments which had previously been whitewashed.

The present occupants, representing a wide range of artistic disciplines from art historians to painters and stage designers, are still selected by a Joint Ministerial Committee, perpetuating the tradition of those former Grand Prix de Rome winners who, like Ingres, Berlioz, Fragonard and Debussy, came to the Eternal City in pursuit of spiritual rejuvenation. Like their forerunners, today's boarders enjoy the rare privilege of wandering freely through the maze of garden paths, seeking inspiration on some stone bench in the shade of the tall pines, walking along the main alley fragrant with the perfume of orange trees and the heady scent of roses, or savouring the Roman skyline glowing in the light of the setting sun from the terrace of the *bosco*. They form the creative leaven of the villa, in their own way, year after year, paying homage to that great patron of the arts, Cardinal Ferdinand de' Medici.

Left hand page, top left
The splendid coffered ceiling of the Chamber of the Elements, nowadays a reception room for guests at the Villa Medici, retraces the birth of the universe after the fusion of its various component elements.

Left hand page, top right
Detail of the vaulted ceiling in the Grand Duchy of Tuscany Room.

Left hand page, bottom left
The painted pergola in Ferdinand de' Medici's pavilion displays his predilection for rare botanical species and exotic fauna.

Left hand page, bottom right
The oriental "Turkish" Chamber, the whim of an early 19th-century Academy Director who had spent time in North Africa.

Opposite
One of the grimacing figures which embellish the enclosure walls.

THE SPLENDOURS OF FRASCATI

Since ancient times, Frascati, standing on the site of the former Roman settlement of Tusculum, had long enjoyed a tradition as a leisure resort. Cato, Cicero and Lucullus were among the fortunate proprietors of the villas scattered on the hillsides surrounding the town. During the Middle Ages, the papacy even managed to wrest the fortress of Tusculum, along with certain feudal rights over the township, from the influential Frascati family, the Colonna. From as early as the 15th century, collectors of antiquities flocked to its ancient ruins.

In 1537, the town, which had been restored to the Colonna a century earlier, was finally sold to the son of Paul III, Pier Luigi Farnese, who transferred it by deed to the papal State. Armed with his new prerogatives, the Farnese pope was able to launch an extensive programme of urban renovation. The major alterations carried out were officially commemorated in 1549 by the striking of a medal which depicted the new town wall and bore the inscription "TVSCVLO RESTITVTO", leaving no doubt as to the papal ambition to restore the town to its former imperial splendour. The Villa Rufina – belonging to Monsignor Alessandro Rufini, bishop of Melfi – became the first in a long series of sumptuous residences which, throughout the 16th and 17th centuries, were to be built on its hillslopes and were to help turn Frascati into the most fashionable resort of the period.

Most of these residences were built on the north slopes of the Alban hills, against the backdrop of the dense screen of oak and chestnut forests which overlook the valley that cradles Rome. In the 16th century, the country houses tended to be little more than small *vigne*, built for utilitarian rather than æsthetic purposes. Each pavilion was provided with a small garden and often embellished with fountains, although seldom boasting jets, as water was a rare commodity in the hills.

With the arrival in Frascati of Cardinal Marco Sittico Altemps, nephew of Pope Pius IV, and with the election of Pope Gregory XIII, a new spate of building works began. In 1567, Cardinal Altemps purchased the Ricci *casino* then commissioned the famous architect Martino Longhi to convert it into a sumptuous villa, which he named Villa Mondragone, in honour of the pope whose coat of arms proudly featured a

dragon. Gregory XIII was a regular guest, faithfully spending each vacation season there. Even the stern Jesuit Cardinal Carlo Borromeo, who took advantage of his friendship with the pope to criticise his excessive fondness for summer resorts, was not averse to visiting the Villa Mondragone in order to discuss ecclesiastical affairs with the pontiff.

For a while, the election of Sixtus V put a halt to papal vacationing at Frascati as the new pope preferred his own Villa Montalto in Rome. The town's fortunes later revived, however, with the arrival, each autumn, of Pope Clement VIII and his nephew, Cardinal Pietro Aldobrandini. In 1597, the Apostolic Chamber acquired the Villa Contugis which the pope offered to his nephew. This modest residence was entirely redesigned by Giacomo Della Porta as the splendid Villa Aldobrandini, and towered over the Frascati hills throughout the 17th century.

The rear façade of the Villa Aldobrandini framed by the twin torsaded columns marking the limit of the wood.

The Villa Aldobrandini

In 1601, Cardinal Pietro Aldobrandini commissioned Giacomo Della Porta, the pupil of Vignola, to design a grandiose villa on the Frascati hills to celebrate the social pinnacle finally attained by his family with the election to the papacy of his uncle, Clement VIII. The cardinal spared no efforts in his project, carving into the hillside to lay out his new residence and ordering the construction of an aqueduct more than five miles long to pipe the spring water from Monte Algido to the numerous fountains that would embellish the villa gardens.

By the sheer extent of its lands, by its imposing size – a veritable palace rather than a country residence – and by its sumptuous decoration which heralds baroque extravagance, the Villa Aldobrandini marks a definitive break with the intimate, restrained character of the Renaissance villa. Its majestic façade, formerly approached via the long alley lined with holm oaks, still looms through the now padlocked gates – of the monumental entrance door on Frascati's main square. Beneath two wide symmetrical ramps, a nymphaeum forms the intermediary level of a vast terrace, enclosed by two walls at the front and the rear. The two ramps, lined by balustrades, and dotted with terracotta pots bristling with box shrubs, form a perfect oval leading to the esplanade in front of the villa.

The triumphantly theatrical setting calls to mind Vignola's somewhat similar approach at the Palazzo Farnese in Caprarola. Surrounded by oak forests, the Villa Aldobrandini

*Previous pages
(pp. 142-143)*
The majestic
main façade
of the Villa Aldobrandini,
with its rows
of small windows.

Overleaf (p. 143)
The Aldobrandini coat
of arms surmounted
by the papal emblem,
following the election
of Clement VIII in the
early 17th century.

towers magnificently over the entire town, pointing resolutely towards that origin of all wordly success – distant Rome, nestling down in the valley against the backdrop of the Tyrrhenian Sea.

Surmounted by a belvedere tower – common to most Latium villas – the austere, massive, unornamented main façade rises on three storeys with row upon row of little windows like so many loopholes. The two, much lower, symmetrical flanking wings, curiously embellished with highly extravagant chimney-stack towers, lead round to a third terrace overlooked by the rear façade of the villa which is of less austere appearance owing to the presence of a projecting central block. To the north and south stretch two small geometrically laid-out woods, planted with impeccable rows of centuries-old plane trees. Nowadays, visitors enter the villa from the rear façade. Its countless rooms still retain priceless wall hangings,

Above
The exedra of the aquatic theatre with its rhythmical niches housing pagan statues amidst a decor of false pumice-stone stalactites, pebbles and moss-covered rock.

Opposite
Detail of one of the polychrome mosaic-work columns standing at the entrance to the wood.

Left hand page, bottom left
A graceful floral deity transformed into a sea goddess in the acquatic theatre.

Left hand page, bottom right
From the two first and second-floor loggias, the owner could look out over the wood stretching away up the hillside.

One of the sumptuous rooms in the villa, decorated from floor to ceiling in typical baroque style.

like the silks featuring decorative Chinese landscapes or the leather stamped with the golden star of the Aldobrandini which embellish two small salons where paintings from the prestigious Aldobrandini collections are hung.

The villa's principal axis continues beyond the spectacular aquatic theatre facing the rear façade and culminates a pair of torsaded columns framing a ramped cascade. Designed by Giacomo Della Porta, who built many of the gushing fountains in the city squares of Rome, and completed by the great baroque architect Carlo Maderno, the aquatic theatre forms a graceful exedra, surmounted by a balustrade which was formerly lined with classical statuary. The façade has a rhythmical row of five large niches faced with mosaic work and carved pumice stone; these niches in turn contain other smaller niches which house statues of mythological sea gods and goddesses. Silvan caryatids flank the niches, dolphins lie at the feet of Neptune and Amphitrite, and jets of water spurt from fountains, the most impressive of which is undoubtedly the central one, which features Atlas bearing the terrestrial globe in his mighty arms. In the heyday of the palace, small dark rooms lay behind the niches, where visitors could refresh themselves, or listen in awe to the amplified roar of the waters pouring down the rock.

To the right, skirting one of the small plane woods where, in summer, large clumps of mauve and pink hydrangea bloom at the foot of the trees, visitors may climb a flight of stairs to the upper terrace of the aquatic theatre. From here, two symmetrical staircases framing the ramped cascade lead to the wood, the entrance to which is signalled by two astonishing columns, covered by multicoloured mosaic work and garlands sculpted in relief, known as the Columns of Hercules. The path continues up the hill beyond these columns, still following the central axis, to the Fountain of the Shepherds (so called because of two statues of shepherds housed in the niches on either side of the main central jet), then finally on to the grand waterfall of the Rustic Fountain.

The sheer splendour of the works carried out at the villa apparently exasperated more than one bigoted cardinal. Cardinal Baronio, for instance, left this furious message on the door of the as yet unfinished building: "For a common mortal, this is more than sufficient." In 1621, on the death of Cardinal Pietro Aldobrandini, the villa passed successively by marriage to the Borghese, the Pamphili, and once more to the Borghese,

Opposite
A portrait of Pope Clement VIII hanging against a background of soft-hued wallpaper.

Previous pages (pp. 148-149)
Cardinal Pietro Aldobrandini's starred coat of arms stylishly incorporated into the mantelpiece.

before finally returning, in the 19th century, to the Aldobrandini who restored it to its original state and still jealously maintain it today. It is now generally closed to the public, and visiting is by appointment only.

Above, and top left hand page
The silk wallpaper is a reminder
of the pronounced 18th-century taste
for chinoiseries.

Opposite
A classical statue of Minerva
from the prestigious Aldobrandini
collection.

151

THE BAROQUE TRIUMPHANT

Above
In this painting by A. Ponthus-Cinier,
the shaded alleys of the Villa Doria-
Pamphili gardens, embellished
with balustrades and fountains,
provide the setting for promenades
and lighthearted *scènes champêtres*.
(Chantilly, Musée Condé).

Above
The façade of the Villa Doria-Pamphili, and the lively chiaroscuro effects created by the projecting bas-reliefs, busts and statuary.

Below
In one of the ground-floor rooms, the walls of which are covered with bas-reliefs and paintings, Bernini's *David* prepares to sling a stone at Goliath.

In the late 16th century, the architect and town planner Domenico Fontana, responsible for the main plan of the streets of Rome, introduced a masterly innovation to Roman garden design with his novel scheme for the Villa Peretti Montalto. By providing a variety of constructions within the villa perimeter and deliberately exploiting the natural ruggedness of the terrain, he was able to lay out the gardens along several different axes. This approach, in its heyday in the opening decades of the 17th century, was successfully adopted at the Villa Borghese, the Villa Ludovisi and the Villa Doria Pamphili. As a result, scenic garden arrangement no longer depended solely on views from the axes of major perspectives, but now involved much greater freedom and variety of scope.

In the latter half of the 17th century, Pietro da Cortona's *Casino* Sacchetti – since demolished – marked a second revolution in villa design. The façade of the *casino* with its numerous curving lines added a different dimension, while the successive flights of stairs introduced a new relationship between villa and garden, as if the former, largely open to the exterior, was stretching out to meet the latter.

These new features were soon being employed in the construction of several imposing villas on the hillsides of Frascati and Rome. Increasingly, the façades of villas were conceived of as showcases intended to highlight pieces of antique sculpture such as statuary, epigraphic inscriptions, and bas-reliefs, which were incorporated into the very structure of the building, the missing sections of which were shamelessly reconstructed.

This type of theatrical display showed off the collection of the villa proprietor in its best light, while coinciding perfectly with the baroque spirit of the age. The composite marquetry produced a vibrant ever-changing interplay of chiaroscuro effects.

Buildings thus tended to be transformed into veritable museums. Entire sections were turned into galleries in which antique objects were exhibited, such as at the Villa Ludovisi which boasted a *casino* full of statuary, or, again, at the Villa Borghese, where Cardinal Scipione's collections were on display in virtually every room in the palace.

The Villa Borghese

In 1608, starting out with a small family *vigna* north of Rome beyond the Aurelian Wall, Cardinal Scipione Caffarelli Borghese, nephew of Paul V, began to extend his property by adding a further six *vigne* in order to build a suburban villa worthy of the name. The architect Flaminio Ponzio was commissioned to build the villa and, on the latter's death in 1613, was succeeded by his assistant Giovanni Vasanzio, an artist of Flemish origin who, in particular, was responsible for its decoration. The architectural structure actually recalls the late Renaissance Roman villa type, and above all the Villa Medici, from which it borrows its main parallelipiped block with arcaded central doorway and twin flights of stairs leading to the garden, as well as the two imposing wings surmounted by belvedere towers.

As at the Villa Medici and at the Villa Doria Pamphili, the façade is inlaid with antique marbles enhanced by stucco frames which girdle the niches, medallions, festoons and pediments. Unfortunately, most of the original forty-four statues, seventy busts and one hundred and forty-four bas-reliefs which decorated the façade have been removed leaving the walls nowadays almost bare. Only a few 17th and 18th-century engravings give us some idea of the lavish ornamentation which once bedecked the façade like a theatre drop, highlighting the chiaroscuro effects.

The space surrounding the villa also features a rigidly geometrical right-angled layout. To the front, a large esplanade is closed by a balustrade surmounted by vases and statuary, while to the rear there is a second open space with a central fountain. The building is flanked by two Italian gardens, whose design is attributed to the baroque architect Girolamo Rainaldi, a pupil of Domenico Fontana. Applying the principles set out by the Jesuit-gardener Giovan Battista Ferrari in his floricultural treatise, Rainaldi planted many of the exotic blooms which were to become typical of the Roman baroque garden: tulips, ranunculae, hyacinths, anemones, fritillaries

Previous pages (pp. 154-155)
The elegant Baroque façade of the Palazzina della Meridiana opposite the twin aviaries in the secret garden at the Villa Borghese.

Page 155, top
The main façade of the Villa Borghese still incrusted with antique pieces, depicted in an anonymous 18th-century painting in the Borghese Gallery.

Opposite
Young Woman with a Unicorn, one of the most famous Raphael portraits in the Borghese Gallery.

Above
This neo-classical temple dedicated to Esculapios was erected in the middle of the romantic lake designed by Asprucci in the late 18th century.

Top left hand page
At a corner on one of the alleys, this imposing monument to the memory of Byron illustrates the romantic vein then prevalent in the villa park.

Bottom left hand page
Canova's masterpiece, his portrayal of the fair Pauline Borghese as victorious Venus, against a backdrop of Baroque decor.

and daffodils were mingled with scented bigarades, the bitter orange trees from which orange blossom water is extracted. Alongside the villa, beyond the first Italian parterre, a long secret garden was laid out, embellished with two baroque aviaries which housed rare birds under their wrought-iron cupolae.

This was the only area of the park reserved for the owner and his guests; indeed, from the very outset the gardens were designed to be open to the public. From the main entrance opposite the Porta Pinciana, visitors take the main alley which is lined by two rows of tall cypresses and offers a magnificent view of the villa's façade. On either side, secondary alleys, named after the trees planted there or the buildings to which they lead – "Juniper Alley", "Elm Alley", "Alley of the Dark Fountains" and so on – run past squares of box hedge, at the corners of which stand the marble heads of mischievous fauns, handsome youths and Greek philosophers. At a bend in one of these alleys, the visitors discover, on their right, a small oval-plan pavilion once used for convivial banquet, whose vaulted ceiling was once embellished with an early 17th-century painting depicting a *Banquet of the Gods*.

To the east of the villa, another area of the park, planted with laurels, is criss-crossed by perpendicular alleys. In the heart of this section Grimaldi built a grand open-air theatre, a semicircular space enclosed by herms, with alternating windows and medallions on the rear wall. The northern zone, cut by valleys, was left in a natural wild state and provided a reserve for many animals, both for species common to Latium, like hare, roe and fallow deer, and for animals from more distant climes, such as ostriches, tortoises and lions. The Borghese were thus the founders of one of Rome's first public zoological gardens.

In the late 18th century, Prince Marcantonio IV Borghese decided to commission Antonio Asprucci to redesign this latter area of the park, while leaving the gardens to the front and the rear of the palazzo intact. Asprucci accordingly designed a new square – known as the Piazza di Siena as it formally resembled the famous square of the Tuscan city – which the prince used as a racetrack for his barbs, Arab horses commonly imported to Italy during the Renaissance. To house the antique statue of Esculapios, Asprucci built a neo-classically inspired temple, erected on an islet in the middle of a small, specially-created lake. In this section of the park, known as the "Lake Garden", the promenade through the various alleys culminates at the islet, which visitors may reach by boat.

Top left hand page
Bordering the Piazza di Siena
– the hippodrome laid out for Prince
Marcantonio Borghese – the
Clock-Tower palazzina seems
to be engulfed by the umbrella pines.

Bottom left hand page
One of the many fountains found
along the alleys through the park.

Above
On the ceiling of one of the first-floor
rooms, this fresco depicting
the allegory of the Arts pays tribute
to Borghese patronage.

Asprucci furthermore rebuilt the interior of the palazzo, re-arranging the layout of the collections. Over a period of twelve years, a team of painters, stucco workers and marble sculptors worked to create a sumptuous decor that retains a touch of rococo refinement and yet provides a foretaste of the neo-classical style. The most spectacular room is no doubt the one which looks out from the top floor of the north façade; its walls, decorated with stucco bas-reliefs, crowned with gilded metal capitals, and medallions in Carrara marble on a mosaic background, all blend in harmoniously with the polychrome floor paving and the fresco on the vaulted ceiling.

Under Prince Camillo Borghese, the pictorial decoration of the first two floors was continued by the Turin architect and celebrated archeologist, Luigi Canina, who sought to develop the various themes suggested by statues in the collection. Bernini's famous *Apollo and Daphne* group thus gave rise to the *Tales of Apollo* painted by Marchetti and Angeletti, while the Egyptian Chamber was designed to house the collection's new pharaonic objects acquired as a result of Napoleon's Egyptian campaign. Indeed, much of Camillo Borghese's fortune derived from his marriage to Pauline Bonaparte, the emperor's sister, a marriage to which he also owed his appointment as Governor of Liguria and his status as Imperial Dignitary. In 1807, obsessed by the idea of extending the villa gardens, Prince Borghese even went as far as to sell to the emperor his priceless collection of antique marbles, thus stripping the façade of its ornamentation.

A century later, the villa was acquired by the State and was turned into a museum. The gardens, sold to the City of Rome, became a public park where Roman bourgeois ladies were soon to be seen riding in their coaches while their husbands attended the horse-races. Rome's equivalent of the Parisian bois de Boulogne was officially designated Parco Umberto I, but the name has never caught on with the countless Romans who still flock to the gardens for their Sunday promenade.

Above, top
The Emperors Gallery, decorated with polychrome marble and embellished with busts of Roman Emperors.

Above, bottom
The garden alleys where Romans flock for their Sunday promenade.

Left hand page
A forceful Bernini statue of Pluto bearing off the hapless Proserpine in his arms, sculpted for Cardinal Borghese.

The Casino Dell'Aurora Ludovisi

Cardinal Alessandro Ludovisi, as soon as he was elected pope in 1621, and had taken the name Gregory XV, had his nephew Ludovico Ludovisi appointed to the rank of cardinal. Within a few months, that sudden increase in income meant that the new cardinal was in a position to acquire the vigne of Capponi, del Nero and Altieri, and before long he had also entered into possession of the Villa Orsini too. These properties were all located in an area just beyond the Porta Pinciana north of Rome. The five existing buildings were conserved, and soon formed the largest vacation residence that baroque Rome was ever to see. The most imposing building, known as the *palazzo grande*, was the former Palazzo Orsini, which constituted the main nucleus of the new Villa Ludovisi.

The villa gardens, usually attributed to the baroque painter Domenichino, are familiar to us from several 17th-century engravings and plans. The main entrance, located at the southernmost tip of the villa perimeter, led to a vast esplanade planted with plane trees in the middle of which stood the Triton Fountain. To the east of the entrance portal, the old Capponi *casino* housed Cardinal Ludovisi's collection of antique marbles. To the west of the esplanade lay a walled garden with Italian parterres, embellished with an aviary. Two huge alleys led off at right angles from the fountain: the first ran in a straight line, traversing a vast box-hedge maze – a kind

of open-air museum in which numerous antique statues were tucked away – then cut across the fields as far as the Aurelian Wall; the second climbed uphill to the old Cecchino del Nero casino which about this time began to be known as the *Casino* dell'Aurora. Stendhal, passing through Rome, was deeply impressed by the ensemble; he could find "nothing more remarkable...than these gardens filled with architecture of which the Tuileries and Versailles are merely pale imitations".

The Casino dell'Aurora, which formerly had two separate north and south entrances, has a cruciform plan and is surmounted by a belvedere tower offering a panoramic view. Originally, the building was surrounded by a circle of antique statues. Each floor is provided with a central room with four smaller rooms branching off along the arms of the cross; on the ground floor, one of the latter rooms serves as a vestibule and still displays the 16th-century grotesque decorations commissioned by Francesco del Nero, apostolic secretary to the pope, and former proprietor of the vigna.

In 1623, Cardinal Ludovisi entrusted two illustrious Roman baroque painters, Agostino Tassi and Il Guercino, with

Left hand page
On the vaulted ceiling of the Aurora Room, Agostino Tassi's daringly designed trompe-l'œil architectural setting highlights Guercino's frescoes.

Opposite
In the *casino* gardens a few statues survive, reminders of a more glorious age.

Previous pages (pp. 162-163)
The rear façade of the Casino dell'Aurora still retains the unobtrusive appearance of a 16th-century country house.

Previous pages (pp. 166-167)
In the centre of the vaulted ceiling
decorated by Guercino, the chariot
bearing Aurora, dressed in red
and white robes, leaps spectacularly
into the void.

the interior decoration. Works got off to a brisk start with the development of selected themes which could be interpreted allegorically to proclaim the auspicious new era ushered in by the election of Gregory XV. Accordingly, the *Fame* fresco on the first floor is a direct echo of the *Aurora* fresco in the central room on the ground floor. Following the method adopted by Pietro da Cortona for the ceiling of the Palazzo Barberini, Guercino took as a theme for the freco the family heraldic motif of triple golden rays set against a red background. Owing to the limited space at his disposal, however, he was obliged to develop his thematic programme vertically on several floors rather than horizontally within a single vast space as at the Palazzo Barberini. From the ground floor to the central tower, crowned by a lantern reminiscent of those seen in the cupolae of Roman churches, the heart of the *casino* resembles a veritable temple erected to the glory of the Ludovisi.

On the ceiling of the ground-floor main room, Agostino Tassi's trompe-l'œil decoration seems to continue the vertical plane of the walls by means of a daring architectonic setting which focusses the viewer's gaze on the central scene in which the horses drawing Aurora's chariot leap forth into the void. On the longer sides of the composition, patches of landscape can be glimpsed through two breaks in the clouds. On the shorter sides lunettes depict the daily solar cycle: the allegory of *Night* features a young woman slumped over her book as she keeps watch over her two slumbering children, Sleep and Death, under the gaze of an owl, while the allegory of day features a triumphant torch-bearing angel. Guercino's main source of inspiration was Cesare Ripa's *Iconologia*, a small compendium of allegories published in the late 16th century which remained immensely popular with artists throughout the 17th and much of the 18th centuries.

Aurora's chariot points in the direction of the spiral staircase which leads to the first floor, and emerges into a room of dimensions comparable to those of the room below. The ceiling of this room features yet another architectural decor, this time designed by Tassi. Here the decor is supported on twin barley-sugar columns, similar to those adopted by Bernini in his baldacchino at St Peter's. The balustrade surmounting the cornice frames the central scene where Fame, a winged allegory in flowing robes holding an olive branch, proudly sounds her trumpet in the direction of a phoenix, the mythical bird which is perpetually reborn. Originally, three sunbeams

Above, and right hand page
These two Dacian prisoners guard
the entrance to the *casino*.

Opposite
Perched on his parapet a lion
jealously stands guard
over the Ludovisi estate.

– no longer visible – shone across the sky, in an allusion to the Ludovisi heraldic emblem. Two further allegories are depicted at the feet of the Fame: Honour, wearing a laurel crown and draped in yellow, and Virtue, dressed in red.

The *casino* is the only building in the villa to have survived intact. Following two new extensions carried out in 1825 and 1851 respectively by Antonio Boncompagni Ludovisi, the villa was effectively demolished by its owners in 1883. On that occasion, much of the property was acquired by the Roman municipal authorities. As new building land was needed, the monumental entrance was knocked down, and the whole aspect of the site was profoundly altered by the levelling of the hill on which the Casino dell'Aurora had stood. A new neighbourhood was created around the Via Veneto, and neither the other buildings, nor the vast gardens of the villa were spared. The centuries-old cypresses and plane trees were felled, and the antiquities were transferred to the collections of the Museo Nazionale Romano. A few of the fountains survived, and they can still be seen today in the gardens of the American embassy, the former Palazzo Margherita which Rudolfo Boncompagni Ludovisi had built towards the end of the 19th century.

The Villa Doria Pamphili

Together with the Villa Borghese, the Villa Doria Pamphili is one of the most majestic of Roman baroque villas. Its four hundred acres of parkland and pine forest rival the finest estates to be found in Latium.

The oldest building on the estate, the *villa vecchia*, features on plans of 17th-century Rome, located at the northernmost tip of the one hundred-acre vineyard acquired by Pamphilio Pamphili in 1630. The Pamphili apparently always used this *casino* as the family residence while the new palace, built farther to the east of the estate after 1644, contained state rooms where the antique collections were displayed. In the space of twenty years, Pamphilio's son, Camillo Pamphili, bought up twenty-three neighbouring plots of vines; that extension to the estate, without which the palace could never have been built, was no doubt greatly facilitated by the election of Camillo's uncle as Pope Innocent X in 1644.

One of the entrance doors giving onto the Via Aurelia led to a long alley where the game of pall-mall – a forerunner of croquet – was played. Crossing a garden planted with tall cypress hedges along which stood a row of statues and busts representing the Twelve Caesars, the visitor reached the majestic "Palace of Statues", also known as the *Palazzo di Belrespiro* because of the mild climate and healthy air.

Innocent X's accredited sculptor, Alessandro Algardi, the representative of a much more classical style which pursued

Above
In this 18th-century painting by C.J.Vernet, gallants whisper sweet nothings to noble Roman ladies in alleys lined by fountains and tall cypress hedges. (Moscow, Pushkin Museum).

Left hand page
The majestic baroque façade of the Villa Doria-Pamphili with the effect of undulating movement created by the projecting central section and the columns in relief.

Previous pages (pp. 174-175)
The vast esplanade with its Italian parterre laid out in front of the "Palace of Statues" forms the second terrace of the park.

greater simplicity, was entrusted with the project. Although Algardi personally designed the meticulously refined and elegantly detailed stucco festoons which embellish the façade, the Bolognese landscape painter Giovanni Francesco Grimaldi was responsible for the actual building of the palazzo. The sloping plot was laid out in three terraces, separated by high walls containing niches and conveniently linked by twin flights of stairs. To the north, the secret garden planted with cypress trees was located on the first level; the palace, together with an Italian parterre laid out around a fountain and flanked by fishponds on either side, stood on the second level; finally, the third level, which began at the Venus Grotto hewn out beneath the flight of stairs, opened out onto a vast stretch of gardens, known as the "theatre gardens" because of the large exedra where all sorts of performances were held. The tiered layout creates a monumental effect of depth, increasing the apparent size of the gardens.

The façade was designed as an elegant showcase intended, as at the Villa Medici or at the Villa Borghese, to highlight

Above
The Lily Fountain, one of two works
by Bernini for the Pamphili, stands
in this clearing in the western section
of the park.

Left hand page
One of the many bas-reliefs from
classical sarcophagi, inlaid like
precious stones into the palace façade.

Opposite
In order to retain the naturally
sloping terrain, Algardi laid
out successive terraces creating
a spectacular change in level
between the front and rear
of the palace.

Above
This nymph emerges from amidst
the foliage along one of the paths
through the wood.

the antique marbles from the Pamphili collection. Bas-reliefs, medallions and statues mounted in niches emphasise the different levels, and create a rhythmic pattern of criss-crossing verticals and horizontals.

The building adopts a compact, Palladian-inspired plan, grouping several rooms around a circular, two-floor high central salon bathed in direct toplight from its vast dome. The apartments were also embellished by statuary framing landscapes of classical ruins. The pictorial decoration designed by Grimaldi, with its personifications of the Virtues and the myth of Hercules, extolled the patronage of Camillo Pamphili and his taste for classical art.

The villa acquired its double-barrelled name in the early 18th century, following a marriage between one of the Pamphilis and a member of the Doria family. At the end of the century, the layout of the parterres was slightly modified, and the Doria eagle was added to the Pamphili lily. The large gardens formerly on the lower level disappeared in the 19th century when, following the marriage of Andrea V Doria Pamphili to Lady Mary Talbot, they were transformed into an English park with winding paths which destroyed the impeccable perspective effect of the ensemble.

Much of the park was given over to botanical gardens while farther to the south a vast area, known as the "Valley of the Deer", was left wild as a natural deer park. The palace is nowadays the property of the Italian State, while the park belongs to the City of Rome.

Left hand page
Beyond the Italian parterre lined by traditional terracotta shrub pots, palm trees mark the edge of the wood.

Below
On the top storey, two winged Victories frame the Pamphili coat of arms surmounted by the pontifical triple crown.

FROM CLASSICISM TO IMPERIAL INTERLUDE

After the splendours of the baroque, the 18th century rediscovered a sense of balance and moderation, and saw the emergence of classicism, a more restrained style which harked back to antiquity. A new feature, this time of Viennese origin, appeared in the gardens – the *Kaffeehaus*, a small pavilion where the Roman bourgeoisie would gather to listen to performances of classical music. Exotic tree species such as magnolia, cedar, sequoia and palms were widely introduced. The arrival of British aristocrats, who married into the great Roman families, often entailed radical changes to the appearance of villa gardens, and traditional Italian symmetry was often replaced by vast green swathes of lawn criss-crossed by winding paths. Romanticism was in the air; in constant pursuit of an idealised past, follies were built and gardens were studded with sham ruins of classical temples such as the Doric Faustina *tempietto* with its partially completed pediment at the Villa Borghese, or Roman theatres and ampitheatres as at the Villa Torlonia.

In the opening years of the 19th century, Pauline Bonaparte, the sister of Napoleon and wife of Prince Camillo Borghese, introduced the fashion for opulently-gilded Empire furniture, obelisks brought back from the Egyptian campaign, and neo-pharaonic frescoes depicting mock hieroglyphs on sombre-tinted backgrounds.

Above
Against a romantic backdrop, Pauline
Bonaparte poses in this portrait
which can be seen in one of the rooms
of her Roman villa.

Opposite
Gregory XVI's 19th-century alterations
to the gardens of the Quirinal Palace
with their impeccable British-style
lawns studded with palm trees
and magnolias.

Above
The elegant elevation of the Quirinal Palace
interior courtyard with its imposing Clock-Tower,
laid out by the two Roman baroque architects,
Carlo Maderno and Domenico Fontana.

Right hand page
Detail of the gilded stucco work on the
sumptuous coffered ceiling of the Pauline
Chapel, commissioned by Pope Paul V
in the early 17th century.

The Palazzo del Quirinale

The Quirinal Palace was the favourite residence of the popes for three centuries, until the arrival of the House of Savoy in 1870 forced them to move to Castelgandolfo. Now the official seat of the Italian Presidency has undergone repeated renovations which, far from altering its personality, have served to enhance it.

Its origins date back to the late 15th century when, still no more than a small *vigna*, it was frequented by all the leading members of the Sacred College of cardinals. Throughout the latter half of the 16th century, the "Vigna di Napoli" – so called because of the Neapolitan origins of its proprietor, Cardinal Oliviero Carafa – enjoyed an outstanding reputation owing to its ideal location on the heights of the Quirinal hill, from where it commands a magnificent panoramic view over the city, and because of the social standing of Cardinal Carafa, who as well as being a great patron of the arts, was also the dean of the Sacred College, and already owned another palace on Piazza Navona. The cardinal no doubt acquired some of the land on which the present-day Quirinal stands following his promotion to the purple in 1467, and he immediately began to develop it, building a small residence with a garden and a vineyard. Maps of late 15th-century Rome suggest that the *vigna* was located in the western part of the present site occupied by the palace.

It was from 1550 onwards, however, when Cardinal Ippolito d'Este had taken over the lease, that the small *vigna*

Left hand page, and above
The palace state rooms, laid out
in the 18th century and decorated
with tapestries, gilding, Murano glass
chandeliers and mirrors,
in a grandiloquently luxurious style
worthy of the Hall of Mirrors
at Versailles.

Opposite
The main façade of the Quirinal Palace
looking onto the square dominated
by the famous classical sculpture
of the Dioscuri.

Above, top
Detail of a candelabra against a backdrop of Chinese silk.

Above, bottom
God surrounded by music-playing angels on the ceiling of the Cappella dell'Annunciata.

Left hand page
Suite of doors in the 18th-century apartments with the spatial effect infinitely multiplied by mirrors.

definitively changed in appearance. The gardens were considerably enlarged, and extended from the rear of the house up the hill slope to the present-day Trevi Fountain. As was the case with the gardens at Cardinal d'Este's other villa at Tivoli, the layout featured a criss-crossing network of lush green parterres planted with espaliered laurels and myrtles, lined with terracotta pots containing citrus-fruit trees, and fancifully embellished with antique statues by designer Pirro Ligorio. The gardens were dotted with pergolas and wooden pavilions overrun by climbing plants, and fragrant blooms and rare species from Turkey and Crete were patiently cultivated by Father Evangelista Quattrini, the resident botanist and head gardener.

In 1584, Pope Gregory XIII issued a decree making the Quirinal palace an official pontifical residence. Over three centuries, and usually for long periods, successive popes lived there, particularly appreciating its reputedly healthy air, despite the fact that twenty-two of the twenty-nine pontiffs who resided there also died on the premises! Following Pope Gregory's decision, the palace was considerably enlarged under the supervision of the architect Ottaviano Mascherino and the hydraulic network supplying the numerous garden fountains was installed, drawing water from the Acqua Felice spring. In the late 16th century, Clement VIII commissioned a new garden layout and the construction of the Organ Fountain – the only fountain to have survived – in which a system of cogs on a water-powered wheel struck on keys and played operatic airs.

The architectural renovation of the palace, however, was undertaken in the early 17th century under Paul V who commissioned two major baroque architects, Carlo Maderno and Domenico Fontana, to design the plan of the present-day building. In accordance with their scheme, a quadrangular structure was laid out around a grand interior courtyard, the front bay of which faces the gardens and is provided with an entrance door and loggia surmounted and continued by a belvedere tower. The palace moreover contains some extremely fine baroque rooms, including the Royal Room and the Pauline Chapel, the latter featuring, on the right hand side of the choir, a tiny secret chamber with a little dormer window from where the pope could attend Mass, concealed from the public gaze.

It was Urban VIII who enlarged the garden to its current dimensions, extending it eastwards to the church of S. Carlo alle Quattro Fontane and enclosing it behind high walls, thus giving it an almost triangular shape. Benedict XIV's positive infatuation with the Quirinal gardens led him to build a fashionable 18th-century *Kaffeehaus* pavilion in the western section where he would spend most of his time, even going so far as to use it for the formal reception of diplomats and pilgrims passing through Rome. At the beginning of the following century, Gregory XVI introduced new exotic trees such as magnolias and Brazilian conifers, planting them in a romantic setting around a Swiss chalet to the rear of the gardens. Gregory also commissioned the last garden maze to be laid out in Italy, an astonishing network of box hedges that form a huge ellipse as they wind in circles around an Egyptian obelisk. Further 19th-century developments included the provision of a fishpond in front of the *Kaffeehaus*, which was embellished by a group of sculptures which formerly stood in the gardens of the royal villa at Caserta, and the introduction of numerous species of palm trees which now stud the English lawns laid out at the same period.

Opposite
The small Cappella dell'Annunciata, nowadays reserved for the use of the President of the Italian Republic, takes its name from the luminous 17th-century altarpiece painting by Guido Reni.

Right hand page
The main state room, known as the Royal Room, with its magnificent coffered ceiling built in the reign of Pope Paul V.

191

The Villa Bonaparte

Although the present-day Villa Bonaparte dates back to the 18th century, an earlier building called the Villa Cicciaporci, located on the Pincio heights at the northernmost limit of the city of Rome features on maps from as early as the late 16th century. The lands form a triangle bounded by the ancient Porta Pia and Porta Salaria, and as with many villas at the time, the estate backed onto the Aurelian Wall, while the villa itself nestled in the far eastern corner. Silvio Valenti Gonzaga, Pope Benedict XIV's Secretary of State, who acquired the property in the mid-18th century, preferred to have a second building, surrounded by gardens, built farther to the west in the centre of the triangular estate. Cardinal Valenti was an outstanding diplomat and a leading figure in 18th century Roman artistic circles. His villa housed a well-stocked library as well as a collection of scientific instruments, silverware, porcelain, and oriental art objects. His famous picture gallery proudly boasts a work by Gianpaolo Pannini, the pre-eminent painter of Roman *vedute*, depicting a group of gentlemen inspecting a project for a building which can only be the Villa Valenti, given the presence on the plan of a flanking ditch surmounted by a balustrade, a specific feature of the villa, and quite unique in the city. This detail would suggest that works on the building commenced around the time the painting was executed, i.e. towards 1749. Pannini may well also have been responsible for the interior decoration.

Except for the statuary and pots which formerly embelli-shed the surrounding balustrade, the villa still conserves its 18th-century exterior appearance. Its compact, almost cubic mass is attenuated on the main façade by a large triple-arched portico surmounted on the *piano nobile* by three large windows set closely together. The classically restrained architecture evokes the Renaissance style rather than the prevailing rococo spirit. The rooms, originally hung with Chinese wallpaper, have been entirely redecorated in a neo-classical vein. The cardinal's passionate interest in physics led him to design the acoustics in the entrance vestibule in such a manner that from each corner the slightest murmur emanating from the opposite end of the room is distinctly audible.

In front of the villa portico were French parterres laid out lined with terracotta pots containing citrus fruit trees and crossed by a large alley which ran from the entrance door. Beyond the parterres, an arcaded box-hedge wall planted alongside the palace led to the small wood and kitchen garden, both located on a slightly higher level. Espaliered lemon and orange trees grew along the Aurelian Wall. The variety of spe-cies grown in the garden aroused the admiration of visitors who, for the first time ever in Rome, were treated to the plea-sant surprise of tasting pineapples.

After the death of Cardinal Valenti in 1756, the villa was bought by Cardinal Prospero Colonna, Benedict XIV's major-domo, and finally, in 1809, it was acquired by Pauline Bonaparte, the sister of Napoleon, who lived in Rome following her marriage to Prince Camillo Borghese. It took the name of its charming new owner: Villa Paolina. Pauline Bonaparte was responsible for the imposing interiors with their Empire fur-nishings, such as the chairs with sphinx-shaped arms and the neo-classical frescoes depicting landscapes with antique ruins, or great female figures from ancient Greek literature (Sappho, Aspasia, Corinna) or from Roman mythology (Atalanta and Hippomenes, Minerva and the Muses, the Judgement of Paris). As a memorial to her brother's Egyptian campaign, she had one of the ground-floor rooms decorated in a neo-pharaonic style featuring hieroglyphs set against a background of Empire green and carmine. A spiral staircase leads to the monochrome-painted first-floor circular salon, where the vaulted ceiling is embellished with mock coffers inspired by the Pantheon dome, and the walls decorated with trompe-l'œil niches framing illu-sionist antique statues of the Muses. Each week at the Villa

Previous pages (pp. 192-193)
The harmonious main façade of the Villa Bonaparte, highlighted by the impeccable symmetry of the fenestration and the arches of the twin-columned portico.

Above
The side façade with its multiple windows which catch the soft morning light.

Left hand page
The garden parterres are studded with magnificent orange trees and framed by tall box hedges.

Previous pages (pp. 196-197)
Top, left hand page
The first-floor gallery
with the decorative trellis on its
vaulted ceiling which opens the space
to the exterior.

Bottom, left hand page
The entrance vestibule,
with its alabaster-white stucco vaulted
ceiling, leads to the ground-floor
rooms and the spiral staircase
to the first floor.

Right hand page
The neo-Egyptian Room, decorated
in carmine and Empire green tones,
celebrates Napoleon Bonaparte's
Egyptian campaign.

Paolina, the princess held dazzling lunches attended by guests of all nationalities and social backgrounds, where British aristocrats and Roman and German princes would rub shoulders with American businessmen in the glittering salons.

On her death in 1825, Pauline bequeathed the villa to her nephew Napoleon Louis and his wife Charlotte. After many vicissitudes, including the destruction by Garibaldi's troops in 1870 of the section of the Aurelian Wall abutting the villa and the loss of some of the land, the property was sold in 1907 by the heirs of Napoleon Charles Bonaparte to the Prussian ambassador, Otto von Mühlberg, who undertook restoration works. In 1951, the Villa Paolina became the official residence of the French ambassador to the Holy See and has been scrupulously maintained ever since.

Above
Detail of the mock hieroglyphs painted on the ceiling of the Egyptian Room.

Top left hand page
The admirable grisaille figures in the first-floor salon which is reached directly via the spiral staircase.

Bottom left hand page
The ground-floor guest rooms display the omnipresent Napoleonic taste.

BY WAY OF CONCLUSION

And so we reach the end of our brief excursion into the world of Roman villas and palaces, of these buildings and parks imbued with the charm, aspirations and grandeur of a by gone age, which encapsulate a marvelous and enviable lifestyle.

This portrait of the Roman palazzi is above all a tribute to the city itself, which has eternally captured the human imagination and given rise to the most extravagant and magnificent of projects. Rome has always been a natural home for all that is splendid and grandiose, and it remains so today.

To tell this story has also been to pay hommage to the men of those times, revealing their ambitions, their dreams of beauty and power, their folly and audacity through the grand architectural schemes they devised and executed. Men of a calibre no longer found, whose noblest virtues were no doubt their sheer enthusiasm and intrepid zeal.

Finally, it is an open invitation to all to embark upon a voyage of enchanting discovery.

The Roman skyline glowing
in the light of the setting sun, seen
from the gardens of the Villa Medici.

PRACTICAL INFORMATION

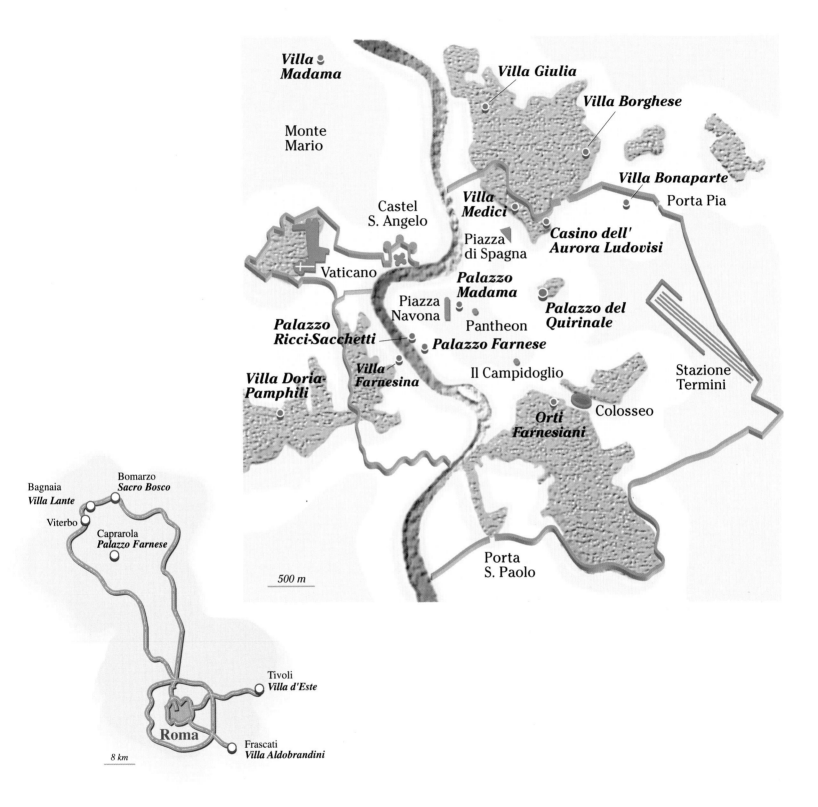

Villa
Madama

Villa Giulia

Villa Borghese

Monte
Mario

Villa Bonaparte

Porta Pia

Castel
S. Angelo

Villa
Medici

Piazza
di Spagna

Casino dell'
Aurora Ludovisi

Vaticano

Palazzo
Madama

Piazza
Navona

Pantheon

Palazzo del
Quirinale

Palazzo
Ricci-Sacchetti

Palazzo Farnese

Stazione
Termini

Villa Doria-
Pamphili

Villa
Farnesina

Il Campidoglio

Colosseo

Orti
Farnesiani

500 m

Porta
S. Paolo

Bagnaia
Villa Lante

Bomarzo
Sacro Bosco

Viterbo

Caprarola
Palazzo Farnese

Tivoli
Villa d'Este

Roma

8 km

Frascati
Villa Aldobrandini

FURTHER READING

ACKERMAN, J.S., *The Villa. Form and Ideology of Country Houses*, Princeton, N.J., Princeton University Press, 1990.

AZZI VISENTINI, M., *La Villa in Italia. Quattrocento e Cinquecento*, Milan, Electa, 1995.

BELLI BARSALI, I. and BRANCHETTI, G., *Ville della campagna romana*, Milan, Rusconi, 1988.

BELLI BARSALI, I., *Ville di Roma*, Milan, Rusconi 1983.

BONOMELLI, E., *I papi in campagna*, Rome, 1953.

COFFIN, D.R., *Gardens and Gardening in Papal Rome*, Princeton, N. J., Princeton University Press, 1991.

COFFIN, D.R., *The Villa in the Life of Renaissance Rome*, Princeton, N. J., Princeton University Press, 1988.

DELUMEAU, J., *Vie économique et sociale de Rome dans la seconde moitié du XVIᵉ siècle*, Paris, 2 vols., 1957-1959.

GUERRINI, P., *Villa e paese. Dimore nobili del Tusculo e di Marino*, Rome, De Luca, 1980.

INSOLERA, S., *Roma*, coll. "Le città nella storia d'Italia", Bari, 1980.

MADER, G. and NEUBERT-MADER, L., *Jardins italiens*, Freiburg, Office du Livre, 1987.

PECCHIAI, P., *Roma nel Cinquecento*, Bologna, Licino Cappeli, 1948.

SALERNO, L., SPEZZAFERRO, L. and TAFURI, M., *Via Giulia*, Rome, 1973.

SHEPHERD, J.C. and JELLICOE, G.A., *Italian Gardens in the Renaissance*, London, Academy Ed., 1986.

SIMONINI, G.L., *Giardini italiani*, vol.2, *Dalla Toscana alla Sicilia*, Milan, Idealibri, 1992.

TOMASETTI, G., *La campagna romana antica, medioevale e moderna*, Rome, 4 vols., 1910-1926.

TORSELLI, G., *Palazzi di Roma*, Milan, 1965.

TORSELLI, G., *Ville di Roma*, Milan, 1968.

ZACCAGNINI, C., *Le Ville di Roma*, Rome, Newton Compton Ed., 1991.

Delicate topiary scrolls at the Villa Lante, Bagnaia.

ACKNOWLEDGEMENTS

In Rome, my project invariably met with keen interest on the part of both French and Italian official bodies and individuals. Apart from a few refusals not worth mentioning, most of the administrative departments and private owners of buildings whom I contacted granted me unlimited access to their property, and graciously accepted both the time constraints inherent in our schedule and the – often numerous! – conditions set by the photographer. I should like here to express my profound gratitude to them all for having shared with me the treasures in their villas and for the unselfish kindness and infinite patience which they showed.

My warmest thanks therefore to: at the Villa Bonaparte, The French ambassador to the Holy See, M. Jean-Louis Lucet and Monsignor Guy Terrancle; at the Palazzo Farnese, the French ambassador to the Italian Republic, M. Jean-Bernard Mérimée, M. Claude Bouheret et Mme Gensollen; at the Villa Madama, Ambasciatore Giulio di Lorenzo Badia and Dott. ssa Di Branco; at the Villa Doria Pamphili, Professor Riondino and Marshal Finazzi; at the Palazzo Madama, Dott. Giovanni Diciommo and Dott. Benizione; at the Palazzo del Quirinale, Dott. Alberto Bruno and Dott. Riparbelli; at the Villa Borghese, Dott. ssa Anna Lobianco; at the Villa Giulia, Dott. ssa Falsini; at the Villa Farnesina, Dott. Donzelli; at the Sacro Bosco, Bomarzo, Dott. Acc. Giovanni Bettini; at the Palazzo Ricci-Sacchetti, Marquis don Giulio Sacchetti and Dott. ssa Loredana Pietrangeli; at the Villa Aldobrandini in Frascati, Prince don Camillo Aldobrandini and Mme Mattioli; at the Casino dell'Aurora Ludovisi, Prince don Niccolo Boncompagni-Ludovisi and Mme Tatiana.

This book could never have been written without the unfailingly amicable support and interest of M. Jean-Pierre Angrémy, Director of the French Academy in Rome, nor without the cordial hospitality of the staff at the Villa Medici, who guided me through the complexities of Roman society. Michel Hochmann, Cristina Galamini, Evelyne Rollet, André Haize and Alessandra Gariazzo, whose familiar presence rendered the whole task that much less daunting, are fully aware of all that this book owes to them.

Opposite
Flying cupids hunting for targets, on the walls of the Alexander and Roxane Room at the Villa Farnesina.

Finally, I would like to pay homage to my faithful colla-
borator Raffaello Bencini, a constant companion whose inces-
sant grumbling and charming humour added spice and pleasure
to my visits to Rome. My sincere thanks also go out to Marcello
Bertoni who so often helped us on our Roman expeditions.

As for the man of my life, he knows that without his daily
support I could have never accomplished this task.

PHOTO CREDITS

All photographs in this book are by Raffaello Bencino excepting:
Archives Pierre Terrail, Paris: pp. 10, 11, 62, 63
Ashmolean Museum, Oxford: p. 24
Agence Diaf, photographer Langeland, Paris: pp. 153, 156, 157, 159, 160, 161
Photographe Gaston, Paris: p. 132
Agence Giraudon, Paris: pp. 133, 134, 152, 155, 157, 173
Agence Hoa-Qui, photographer Grandadam, Paris: p. 154.

Imprimé en Italie
La Zincografica Fiorentina